SUNDAY IS MY DAY

SUNDAY IS MY DAY

REVEREND IRVING FRYAR

MULTNOMAH PUBLISHERS
Sisters, Oregon

SUNDAY IS MY DAY
published by Multnomah Publishers, Inc.

© 1997 by Irving Fryar

Cover photograph by Photo File, Inc., Yonkers, New York
Cover design by Left Coast Design

International Standard Book Number: 1-57673-225-8
Printed in the United States of America

Scripture quotations are from:
The Holy Bible: New International Version (NIV) ©1973, 1984 by
International Bible Society. Used by permission of Zondervan Bible Publishers.

For information:
Multnomah Publishers, Inc., PO Box 1720, Sisters, Oregon 97759

97 98 99 00 01 02 03 — 10 9 8 7 6 5 4 3 2 1

To my wife, Jacqui,
and to my children:
Londen Aaron, Irving Dale Jr.,
Adrianne Mertice, and Jacqueline Taylor Monique

TABLE OF CONTENTS

Acknowledgments

I would like to thank the following people for the impact they've made on my life:

Bill Gordon, Tom Osborne, Frank Solich, Dean Huey, Raymond Berry, Don Shula, and Ray Rhodes.

Pastor Charles and Elwina Terry from the Greater New Birth Baptist Church in Plano, Texas; Pastor William and Louella Dickerson from the Greater Love Tabernacle Ministries in Boston, Massachusetts; Pastor Robert and Alene Stanley from the Hopewell Missionary Baptist Church in Pompano Beach, Florida; and Minister Tony Anderson.

Ronnie and Sheryl Lippett, Michael and Edwena Timpson, Michael and Christine George, Pastor Joe Guadanino, and Craig and Mary Kaplan.

And thanks especially to Mom and Dad and my two sisters, Faith and Hope.

INTRODUCTION

Do you want to see a happy man? Do you want to see a man who has every reason in the world to be grateful? Do you want to see someone who gets up every morning thankful for another day?

If you do, take a look at me.

I'm a happy man because I'm doing what God wants me to do. I'm spreading the good news of salvation through Jesus Christ, both as a player in the National Football League and as a preacher during the off-season.

It is because of the grace and mercy from the heavenly Father that I'm a happy man. It's because of the Lord Jesus Christ.

It wasn't always that way for me. There was a time when I was as far away from God and His ways as could be. I was walking in disobedience to God, rebelling against what He wanted from me. At that time in my life, nobody could have guessed that one day I'd be the "Reverend" Irving Fryar.

By the world's standards, I was living a dream. I had it all—money, jewelry, expensive cars and houses, clothes, fame. I was a millionaire with a beautiful wife and kids, and a job that put me in front of tens of thousands of adoring fans every Sunday afternoon. I had the best of everything. From the outside looking in, it appeared that I had everything any man could want in life, and more.

Outside appearances can be deceptive, though, and mine certainly was. In spite of everything I had, I was the most miserable person in the world. I was angry, lonely, depressed, confused, isolated. You name a negative emotion and it was inside me, eating me up day after day, making my life hell on earth.

I was so miserable that I literally wanted to die. In fact, I tried to take my own life on more than one occasion. Despite all that I had, I had gotten to the point where I couldn't see any sense in going on. So I tried to end it all. It was only through the grace of God that I survived my attempts at self-destruction.

I tried everything I could to quiet the storm that was raging within me. I tried alcohol. I tried drugs. I tried friends. I tried material possessions. If there's something I could have tried to make myself happy, I tried it over and over. But none of that stuff worked. In fact, some of those things only made it worse.

I needed something more than the pleasures of the world. I needed something deep inside me, something to give my life meaning and give me the peace of mind and calmness of spirit that I couldn't find in the world.

I needed Jesus.

I needed to quit running, call on the name of the Lord Jesus Christ, and acknowledge His calling on my life to preach, a calling I received when I was a teenager but ran from because I thought preachers were boring people.

I ran from God's calling for years. But He wouldn't let me go. He followed me with that calling to the University of Nebraska, where I was an All-American on the Cornhusker football team, then to the National Football League, where I was the number-one pick in the 1984 draft. He followed me until He finally got me in a place where I had nowhere to look but to Him.

When I finally gave up and let God take control of my life, He started to bless me in ways I never thought possible. He blessed me with inner peace, love for others, joy, and direction in my life. He blessed me with a desire to see others come to know Him as I had and to love the kind of life He's taught me to live.

If you've heard or read anything about me in the past, you probably know that I had a reputation as a bad guy during my first few years in the National Football League. Some of the things that were said about me were true, and some were only partially true. Others weren't true at all. All that aside, though, my life was a mess. I wasn't living right, and my lifestyle was a pathway to destruction. I wasn't necessarily a bad person, just a confused young man who needed the Lord Jesus Christ in his life.

My wife doesn't like it when I talk about the things I've done and the things we've been through. Those were rough times for her, too, and she'd like to keep those things in the past. In one respect, she's absolutely right. Those things are in the past and under the blood of Christ, never again to be remembered by God the Father. But at the same time, they are as much a part of my testimony as playing professional football, and they are proof of what

God can do when we let Him take over.

I don't want to glorify the things that I did in my past, but I also don't want to hide them in shame and act like they never happened. I'm not proud of the mistakes I've made, but at the same time I wouldn't change anything at this point in life. Why? Because I know that God can take the things I've done and use them to bring others to Himself.

I've lived on all sides as far as my relationship with God is concerned. I've lived in total rebellion toward God, not willing to acknowledge Him in any way in my life. I've lived in a halfway, lukewarm relationship with Him. And I've also lived in total surrender to Him, having given Him my mind, body, and soul to do with as He pleases.

I'm a living witness, a human testimony to the power of God to change a man and give him direction in life. I can speak with authority on what it's like to walk away from God, to walk nearer to God, and to walk with God. And I can say with absolute certainty that there's no better life than the one where you walk in that intimate, loving relationship with the heavenly Father, knowing that He cares for you and is pleased with the life you're living for Him.

There's nothing better than the assurance I have in walking with Christ, that assurance that I find in my favorite verses in the Bible, Romans 8:38–39: "For I am convinced that neither death nor life, neither angels nor demons, neither the present nor the future, nor any powers, neither height nor depth, nor anything else in all creation, will be able to separate us from the love of God that is in Christ Jesus Our Lord."

God gave me a high calling in my life: to preach His Word. But it wasn't until I got demoted that I got promoted. I had to go through some hard times before God picked me up, cleansed me, and gave me the opportunity to minister to others as both Irving Fryar the football player and as the Reverend Irving Fryar.

That is my platform, and I want to use it to show people how God can take even the most messed-up life and make something good out of it, how He can redeem our wasted years and use them to bless others who are where I once was, or who may be headed that direction.

The 1997 NFL season is my fourteenth in the league, which is a pretty long run in pro football. I don't know how much longer I'll play, but I know that God has blessed me with some of my best professional seasons over the past four years. Only God knows how much longer I'll play, but I know that as long as I am putting on an NFL uniform on Sunday afternoons God will use my presence on the field to glorify Himself and bring others into His kingdom.

I call this book *Sunday Is My Day* because it's the day God has given me to glorify Him most at this point in my life. The Bible says in Exodus 20:8 to "Remember the Sabbath day by keeping it holy." For most Christian denominations, Sunday is the Sabbath, the Lord's day. Every day of my life belongs to God, but He has given me Sunday to play football during the season and to preach when I'm not playing. And I've learned that I can point people to Him by doing either.

My goal in writing this book is to offer a challenge. That challenge is to give your life, your body, and yourself to the Lord Jesus Christ to do with as He pleases and to live a life that is wholly committed to Him and what He wants you to do. And I'm going to challenge you to do it now and not later. There are no guarantees concerning how long you will have to yield to God. Proverbs 27:1 says, "Do not boast about tomorrow, for you do not know what a day may bring forth."

I want you to be entertained and blessed by my story as you read this book. But more than that, I want to challenge you to totally give God one thing:

Yourself.

CHAPTER ONE

'YOU'RE TOO OLD, IRVING'

A CHALLENGE

The local papers called it "A day for the ageless" and a "career day."

There's no doubt that Sunday, October 20, 1996, was a special day for me. It was a day when everything seemed to go right, a day when every move I made led to something good.

It was the day my team, the Philadelphia Eagles, met my former team, the Miami Dolphins, in a National Football League game at Veterans Stadium in Philadelphia. I had been looking forward to playing the Dolphins that season. A player always wants to do well against his old team, but today I had added motivation. I wanted to show the Dolphins—in particular, Coach Jimmy Johnson—that letting me leave Miami as a free agent following the 1995 season was a mistake.

I'd been having a good year catching passes from Ty Detmer, the fifth-year quarterback from Brigham Young University. He stepped in after Rodney Peete was injured early in the season and had the best season of his career. We subsequently established ourselves as one of the best quarterback-receiver tandems in the league. One publication even compared us to the Steve Young-Jerry Rice duo in San Francisco.

On that day against the Dolphins, though, it was more than just a quarterback and a receiver having a good day together. Ty and I could do no wrong. If I got open, the ball was there for me, and when Ty got it there, I made sure it was a catch. It seemed like the Miami defense was helpless against us.

By the time the game was over, I had eight receptions for 116 yards and a career-high four touchdowns. The touchdowns came on passes of 38, 2,

12, and 36 yards and accounted for twenty-four of our thirty-five points. I found out later that those four scores also tied an Eagles' team record that was set by a couple of guys I'd never heard of: Ben Hawkins against Pittsburgh in 1979, and Joe Carter against Cincinnati in 1934.

Most importantly, though, we won the game 35-28 to improve to 5-2 and send the Veterans Stadium fans happy in the knowledge that their Eagles were still in the chase for the National Football Conference Eastern Division championship.

As for me, I had mixed feelings about how I played. On one hand, it felt good to have played so well and won, and to have shown the Miami coaches that maybe they should have given a little more thought to re-signing me at the end of the 1995 season. But at the same time, I still had some emotional ties to the Dolphins, to the friends who still played for them. Don't get me wrong, if I were to play the Dolphins again, I'd be happy if I could catch ten passes instead of eight and score five touchdowns instead of four. That's my job. But what made that day a little bittersweet was that there was so much talk about it being a "revenge game" for me, and I wasn't into getting revenge on my old Dolphin teammates.

One Great Day, One Great Year

The Miami game was my best day in one of my best seasons in my thirteen years in the NFL. It was a season in which I was able to set the Eagles' team record for pass receptions in one season with eighty-eight and a season in which I had a career high in touchdown catches with eleven. I was also honored as Philadelphia's Offensive Most Valuable Player.

In 1996 my name was put among the all-time receiving greats in the NFL by moving into the career top twenty in both receptions and receiving yards. I finished the season with 650 receptions, good for eleventh all-time, and 10,111 yards to finish the year thirteenth in that category. I passed some great receivers—Hall of Famers, many of them—on both lists, guys like Fred Biletnikoff, Harold Carmichael, Charley Taylor, and my former coach with the New England Patriots, Raymond Berry.

I well remember the day I passed Raymond on the all-time list for receptions. It was in our December 1 game against the New York Giants at Veterans Stadium. I caught six passes to move to eleventh place on the all-time receiving list with 636, three catches ahead of Raymond.

I have nothing but respect and appreciation for what Raymond Berry has done for me and for the game of professional football. He did more to help me achieve what I have in the NFL than anybody. And he stuck by me during my days in New England—the days I now call "the Mess." If it weren't for him, I'd probably have been out of football long ago. But it felt great to pass him, simply because he was one of the greatest receivers to ever play the game, as his spot in the Hall of Fame demonstrates. I haven't had a chance to talk to him since then, but I can't help but think that he was happy for me when I passed him.

I had plenty of other personal highlights in 1996. I had one stretch of three games—the first being the Miami game—in which I had twenty-four receptions for 379 yards and five touchdowns. During that span, I became the first Eagles wide receiver to have three straight 100-yard games since Mike Quick in 1985. I closed that three-game streak by matching my career high in receptions with nine, against the Dallas Cowboys.

Washed Up at 34?

The 1996 season was a great one for me, one in which God blessed me with what many people thought was a career year. But what was amazing about the year I had is that all these things happened to a wide receiver who had been called "too old" and "washed up" prior to the 1996 season. When I signed my contract with the Eagles in the spring of 1996, several Philadelphia-area writers, citing the fact that I would be turning thirty-four early in the season, suggested that signing me was a mistake. Most of them felt that I could contribute something that season. After all, I still could run and catch, and I've always had a reputation as a strong blocker from the wide receiver position. But could I be a much-needed key cog for the Eagles' offense? It didn't seem likely. At least not in the writers' eyes.

Much that was written and said during the 1996 preseason suggested that I was too old to be a key player for the Eagles. Although I was coming off a three-year stint with the Miami Dolphins in which I caught 199 passes for more than 3,000 yards, it seemed like some of the local writers expected me to just burn out when I came to Philadelphia.

While I didn't appreciate someone saying I was too old to play, I didn't get angry. I got motivated. To me, being called "too old" was a challenge I was eager to take on during the coming season.

Actually, I've always been the kind of person who thrives on personal challenges. One of the most memorable was several years ago when I was still with the Patriots. Television analyst Cris Collinsworth, a pretty good receiver during his days with the Cincinnati Bengals, said during a broadcast that I was "washed up" and on my way out of the league. This was at the time when I was getting my life cleaned up after several years of the junk that everybody knew about.

The Bible tells me that I've got to forgive people when they say or do things against me, and I've forgiven Cris for what he said. It still motivates me to think that Collinsworth didn't think I could play any more.

It was the same during the 1996 season. I saw what had been written about my age, and I heard the things people were saying. So I did what I've always done. I went out to prove them wrong.

I like to take on personal challenges and disprove people who doubt me. That's always been a side of me that has helped me to excel during my football career. But while I might be challenged and motivated by the doubts of other people, my biggest motivation isn't what other people say, but Who I know.

Since I've Known Jesus

Some people might think it's simplistic to think of it this way, but when I look at my NFL career, I see a tale of two Irving Fryars. God not only cleansed me, saved me, and gave me a new life when I turned to Him for salvation, but He renewed and rejuvenated what to that point could only have been called just an "OK" career.

The numbers tell that story.

From my rookie year in 1984 to my seventh season in 1990—these were the tough years in my life—I averaged thirty-four catches for 560 yards and a little over four touchdowns a season. Those aren't necessarily bad numbers—in fact, I had better than 800 yards in 1990—but much more was expected of me, largely because I was the first player picked in the 1984 draft. There's no question about it: I was underachieving during those years.

There are a couple of reasons for that, I think. One of them is that there was little or no stability at the quarterback position with the Patriots back then. During those seven seasons between 1984 and 1990, I played with six different quarterbacks. (In fact, I think I have some kind of NFL record for catching passes from the most different passers during a career. Since I came into the league, I've caught passes from sixteen different quarterbacks and two running backs, for a grand total of eighteen passers.) Some of them were good quarterbacks—Steve Grogan and Tony Eason had some great years in New England—but a receiver needs that consistency in his quarterback. I've always said I'd run routes and catch passes from anybody—just give me some consistency in who that somebody is.

There was another reason for my lack of productivity during those years: I had a lot of garbage in my life. It was filled with drugs, lies, fights, and scandals. Looking back on it, there's no way that didn't affect me, if only mentally.

Since I've had a personal relationship with the Lord Jesus Christ, not only has my marriage and the rest of my personal life gotten better, but my play on the football field has given me the reputation as one of the NFL's best receivers.

From the 1991 season through 1996, I've averaged better than sixty-eight catches, 1,031 yards, and six touchdowns a season. Over the past seven seasons, I'm one of only two receivers in the NFL—the other being the great Jerry Rice of the San Francisco 49ers—to record better than fifty receptions each year.

I don't tell you those things to brag, but to give the glory to God for giving me the ability to play football of that caliber. It is through His power that I've found the success I have during the past six seasons. By all the laws of nature, I should be slowing down by now. My body should be giving out, and I should be either just a spot player or out of the NFL entirely.

What really amazes me is how I was able to play in the NFL at all at such a late age. When I look back on the things I was doing back during "the Mess," I see a young man who was on a fast track out of the league. I wasn't living a life that was conducive to a long career in professional sports. I don't know of anybody else who was doing what I was doing back then who is still around. In fact, most of them were out of the league within four or five seasons.

Yet here I am, playing NFL football better each year I'm in the league. James Collins, the Philadelphia Eagles' trainer said I am "a freak of nature," because the older I get the better I seem to play. How can that be, you ask? How can I keep improving when other guys my age are kicking back and drawing their pensions? How can I go out as a 34-year-old man—and believe me, that's pretty old in the world of National Football League wide receivers—and set team records and personal career highs?

While I still do work out hard to keep myself in shape, I'm not doing anything I wasn't doing five years ago. The plain truth is this: It isn't me! It's not by my own strength—not by any stretch of the imagination. It's because of Christ dwelling in me that I'm doing the things I am. It's because God has a purpose for me still being in the NFL.

Physically, I'm still the same Irving Fryar I was before I met Christ, just a little older (and a little wiser). But now I have a purpose in my play that goes beyond getting to the Super Bowl or making a lot of money or getting personal accolades. I not only have a new purpose, but a new confidence that as long as God has me playing in the National Football League, He'll take care of everything.

Before I gave my life to Jesus, I used to worry about a lot of things. I worried about getting hurt. I worried about how well I was playing and if my team would want me back if I didn't produce enough. I had no confidence in myself or in anybody, and I was motivated by fear.

But now that I have Jesus, I'm motivated by faith. It doesn't matter to me what my opponents are doing or how I'm feeling, because God is on my side and I know I'm going to go out there every game and get it done. I have no fear now. I'll run across the middle, where only the most brave-hearted—or foolish—receivers will go, and I'll make the catch. It doesn't matter who's there, because I know that God is with me, and He will keep me healthy and strong for as long as He needs me to play football.

Sometimes, the way things happen on the field shows me beyond any doubt that God is in me, helping me to do things that I couldn't do before. It's almost like the plays happen in slow motion, because they're so easy. And when I score a touchdown or make another great play I kneel or I point to the sky to let people know that it's not me, but God Who gets the glory.

How Long?

I don't know how much longer I'm going to play in the National Football League. I know that Charlie Joiner played eighteen years, and Art Monk played sixteen. Drew Hill and Don Maynard played fifteen apiece, and Fred Biletnikoff, Harold Carmichael, and Steve Largent each played fourteen. Henry Ellard, who is fourth in all-time receiving yardage and third in receptions coming into the 1997 season, played his fourteenth season with the Washington Redskins in 1996 and he was still productive, leading his team in receptions and receiving yardage!

When my current contract with the Eagles expires, I will have played fifteen years. Whether I play any more beyond that is God's call and His alone. Either way, I'm a blessed man. I'm playing professional football and bringing the message of Jesus Christ to people I play with and the people who come to see me play.

My number one priority in whatever I do is to see that people have a chance to know Jesus Christ. That isn't just something I want to do because of my love for Him and for people. It also happens to be my calling.

That calling—one I received when I was just a kid—is what keeps me going.

CHAPTER TWO

THE DAYS OF MY YOUTH
RECEIVING MY CALLING

was only seventeen years old, still trying to figure out what I wanted to be when I grew up—*if* I grew up—when my grandmother, Alice Oakman, said something to me that was destined to have a profound influence on my life. And it had nothing to do with football.

"You know, Irving, God wants you to preach. He's put a call on your life, and you're going to be a preacher."

Call it what you want—a prophecy, a word of knowledge, or just some grandmotherly inkling—Grandma spoke those words with a sincerity and conviction that made me listen to her.

Although I wasn't walking with the Lord at the time, there was something inside me that told me, almost like an audible voice, "Irving, your grandma's right. You're going to be a preacher." Don't ask me how it came to me, but God let me know that He would give me sermons to preach and that people were going to come to know Him through my preaching. A couple of preachers I met when I went to church even told me that I'd be a good preacher. It was as if God was using them to confirm what I already knew.

I loved my grandmother very deeply, but I didn't want to hear about this preacher stuff. I even told her, "Grandma, leave me alone about preaching!" But she couldn't leave me alone about it. Her love for Jesus and her love for me compelled her to tell me the truth as she saw it. I was called to be a minister of the gospel of Jesus Christ.

Grandma brought up the subject of preaching to me many times after that. I didn't like hearing it later any more than I liked hearing it the first time, but I listened respectfully. If there was anybody in my life who could talk to me like that, it was Grandma.

This beautiful, godly woman whom my sisters and I called "Gramere" was a stabilizing influence in my life from the time I was a baby. She was there for all of us during the toughest times when my home life wasn't everything I would have wanted it to be.

A Rough Start

I was born and raised with my two sisters, Faith and Hope, in a section of Mount Holly, New Jersey, that I would now say was just a little better than poor. Both of my parents worked long and hard just to keep the rent paid and food on the table.

There's no doubt in my mind now that my father and my mother loved me as I was growing up and that they did the best they could under some very tough, trying circumstances. But the pressures of taking care of the family took a toll on Mom and Dad's marriage and on their relationship with us kids, and that made things tough on all of us.

My mother was tough on me when I was a kid. She had to be. Dad worked days at a pipe foundry and nights making deliveries for the family-owned dry cleaning business. He wasn't home much, so Mom was the one who had to discipline me. Mom also worked, and she took care of us the best she could. I got more than my share of whippings and I didn't enjoy getting punished like that, but I've come to realize that my mother was doing all she could to provide me with some sort of discipline in my life.

God has allowed me to understand that our family's situation was tough on everybody. Although my father was not at home much, and he did not spend much time with me, at least he was there. He came home at night, unlike the fathers of many of my friends. As an adult, I'm able to look back on that with gratitude.

I also credit my parents for giving me a knowledge of God. I grew up knowing there was a God, and I knew who He was from what I learned in church. God was a big part of my family's life in many ways. We went to church, and my dad sang in a traveling gospel group and my mother was a believer. My sisters both sang in the church choir. I sang in the choir and was a junior deacon at our church in Mount Holly.

Although I went to church regularly, I was never taught how to live a Christian life and how to walk in a relationship with the Lord Jesus Christ. I didn't understand the Bible or what was in it, and I didn't understand what it had to do with my personal life. Somehow, I just understood that God wanted me to live a good life and that going to church was a good thing.

What I did learn from going to church was a sense of right and wrong, and that would turn out to be an important factor in my life later on. Proverbs 22:6 says, "Train up a child in the way he should go, and when he is old he will not depart from it." This proved to be so in my life. Going to church gave me something of a spiritual foundation. Although I rebelled against these things for a time, I never forgot them.

Seeing God in Grandma

I didn't have much of an understanding of what my relationship with God was supposed to be like, but my grandmother certainly did. In many ways, Gramere was the spiritual strength in our family.

Gramere lived across the street from us and always took good care of us. When Mom was away working, Grandma would babysit. We loved being at Grandma's house, a place where we felt the love that only a godly grandmother can give.

Gramere loved having her grandkids over. She took especially great joy in cooking for us, then just sitting and watching us eat. (I think that's a trait my own mother picked up. She also loves to cook and takes great pleasure in seeing others enjoy the meals she prepares.) She just loved making things better for us.

The best meals I ever had with my grandma came from something that she and I had made into our own little tradition. My grandma believed that if the first person she saw on New Year's morning was a man, then it would be a good year. I always wanted my grandma to have a good year, so I made sure I was the first person she would see on New Year's Day. Ever since I can remember, I got up bright and early on New Year's Day and went across the street to Grandma's house. She'd fix a masterpiece of a breakfast, and we'd sit and eat together and enjoy one another's company.

The thing I remember most fondly about Gramere was her voice. She loved to sing, and whenever she was cooking, cleaning, doing laundry, or making her special sun tea, she'd be sweetly singing old-fashioned spirituals, her favorite (and my most memorable) being an old song titled, "Call Him By His Name." Her voice was just as soothing and sweet when she spoke as it was when she sang, even on those occasions when she scolded me.

I had a very special relationship with Gramere. I never acted up when I was around her. I loved her so much that I never wanted her to be unhappy with something I had done. She recited Bible verses to me often, even during the times when I wasn't as interested in the Word as I should have been. She often talked to me of a heavenly Father who loved me more deeply and unconditionally than I could understand.

That day she first told me that I was called to be a preacher was the most memorable and life-changing conversation about God I ever had with my grandmother.

But I didn't want to hear or think about preaching.

For one thing, I was having too good of a time doing the things I did as a kid, and I didn't want to be bothered with thoughts of becoming a preacher. So I either fought the idea of being called, or I simply tried not to think about it.

I had my own ideas of what a preacher's life was like, and I didn't want my life to end up like that. I thought preachers were boring people who couldn't have any fun, couldn't spend time with friends, laugh when something was funny, go to movies, or play sports. As I saw it, being a preacher meant there was a long list of things I couldn't do. I thought all preachers did was sit around their houses reading the Bible all week, then preach on Sunday morning. To me, a preacher's life could be summed up with one word—BORING! I wanted no part of that.

Another thing was that I had a different goal for life—to be a jet pilot in the United States Marine Corps. I always wanted to fly, and I had two uncles who had been in the Marines, so I decided I would be a pilot in the Marine Corps after I graduated from high school. This was long before I'd even thought about playing football in college or had any idea that I could play in the pros.

A G-Town Boy

Most people would look at the life I was leading during my high school days and conclude that God had called someone else to preach and that Grandma mistakenly thought He was talking about me. I attended church with my mother in Mount Holly and even sang in the choir, but I was anything but a "choirboy." I played high school football and baseball, attended church, and got pretty good grades in school, but I was also a member of G-Town (short for "Ghetto Town," a group of street kids who walked around our neighborhood looking for trouble).

When you think of the word *gang* in the context of the 1990s, you wouldn't usually think of G-Town. We thought of ourselves as tough guys, and we got into more than our share of fights, but we didn't carry guns, and we never did a "drive-by" on one of our rivals. Mostly, we hung out together, got in fights (some of them involved knives and lead pipes, although, thankfully, no one was ever killed or seriously injured during one of our fights), and committed what could be considered acts of petty theft.

I don't necessarily think that we were bad kids. I think we were basically good kids with little or no direction from our families and way too much time on our hands. Consequently, we made some bad choices and got involved in some bad activities.

My mother was very strict with me so my affiliation with G-Town didn't get going until my high school years. Mom made sure I was home at night. When the street lights came on, I had to be in the house. If there was one place I was sure to stay out of trouble, it was at home.

Things began to change by the time my sophomore, junior, and senior years in high school rolled around. A lot was going on in Mom's life that I didn't understand. Mom and Dad were having marital problems, and the stress of those problems along with trying to work and take care of us kids got the best of Mom, and she wound up in the hospital with a variety of physical problems.

With Dad and Mom both away from home, I was pretty much on my own. I cooked for myself, washed my own clothes, and did pretty much what I wanted to. That's when I started hanging out with Captain, Bones,

Ace, Jinx, Moose, Wimpy, and the rest of the G-Town guys. They called me "Swift." I wasn't a high man in the G-Town hierarchy, but I started more than my share of trouble because I was a hothead who was always looking for a fight, whether I was at school, at football practice, or hanging out with my friends. I was an angry young man with a quick temper, and I was always looking to fight whoever, wherever, and for whatever reason I could find. If there wasn't a reason, I'd come up with one.

Someone Was Watching Over Me

I may have been on my own as far as family was concerned, but I can see, looking back, that God was always there. There's no other way to explain how I got through those days in G-Town before going on to the University of Nebraska, and finally to the NFL. Nor is there another way to explain how I lived long enough and stayed out of enough trouble to have a chance to acknowledge the calling that God put on my life.

It seems miraculous that I was never seriously hurt when I was running with my G-Town friends because we got ourselves into some situations where, frankly, we could have gotten ourselves killed. Even when I wasn't so much as acknowledging that He existed, and I was walking in direct disobedience to Him, He was protecting me and going before me every step of the way.

One incident in particular stands out which demonstrates this. One night when I was hanging out with the G-Town guys, the eight of us got in a confrontation with another gang—one with about forty members. I don't know why they didn't just jump us then and there because they certainly had the advantage in numbers. However, I got into a one-on-one fight with one of them. We started wrestling around, and the next thing I knew, we were flying through the plate glass window of a Mount Holly pizza parlor. I went through the window first, with this guy right on top of me. And it's a good thing that he was on top of me, because his body shielded me from the flying shards of glass. Other than a few cuts on my face and a few scratches, I wasn't hurt. The other guy walked away with some nasty cuts, some from the glass and one from one of my G-Town friends.

There were other times when I went out at night looking for trouble, only to find none. I can't help but think that God, looking ahead and knowing what I would one day become, kept me out of the very trouble I was looking for.

I also did well to keep myself out of trouble with the law when I was hanging with the G-Town gang. If God had blessed me with anything at that time in my life, it was a measure of common sense. I knew better than to do something that would get me arrested (or if I did something that bad, I knew not to get caught). But there was more to it than that. Somewhere inside me was a God-given conscience. Sure, I'd done a lot of things that I knew were wrong, but there was that voice inside me—that sense of right and wrong—that kept me from going too far. Unlike some of the other kids I was with who have had a lifetime of trouble with the law, I had a sense of limits in my life. I liked the life I was leading, and I liked being seen as a tough guy. But there was something inside me that kept me from stepping over the line that would have sent me into the criminal justice system.

Grandma knew about these things. She may not have known the details of what I was doing, but she knew I wasn't living right. So she did the thing that I know kept me safe. She prayed. I still believe that Grandma's prayers kept me from getting into major trouble. No doubt it was during those prayers that God let Grandma know that I was going to preach.

Running Away

I didn't know what kind of influence God could have on my life and, frankly, I didn't really care. I just wanted to do what I wanted to do—hang out with my friends, party, and play football. I wanted to have fun. I wanted to eventually fly jets in the military. I wanted to live my life the way I saw fit.

But deep down I knew God had another plan, a plan I wanted no part of. So I ran.

I started running, and I didn't stop. Like Jonah fleeing to Tarshish after God called him to preach to the people of Nineveh, I fled to nowhere in particular, trying to leave behind me a calling that was as sure back then as it is today. I ran as fast as I could and as far as I could—just to get away from the calling God had placed on my life.

I don't know if you've ever had God get after you, but when He calls you to do something, there is nowhere you can go to get away from His calling. You can run to the most remote corner of the earth and God will be there. You can run until you turn your life into total chaos and God will be waiting for you. You can run until you are physically, emotionally, and spiritually empty, and God's calling for you will still be sure. And He'll never let you forget that you've been called.

When you run from God, you won't go anywhere but down. The Bible says that when Jonah fled to Tarshish, he went *down* to Joppa, and went *down* into the boat. Later, when the storm came and nearly sunk the boat, Jonah went *down* into the water and *down* into the fish's belly.

When I decided to run from God's calling, I headed down. It took me years before I reached bottom, and not everything that happened to me in the meantime could be seen as bad. But there was no mistaking what direction I was heading. I was running away from God and toward my own destruction.

Just as God followed Jonah onto the boat, into the sea, and then into the belly of the fish, He followed me. He followed me from Mount Holly to Lincoln, Nebraska, where I played football for the Cornhuskers. From there, He followed me through my football career to the jail cell where finally I said, "Enough!" and called out to Him to change me and clean up the mess that my life had become.

When I finally turned to God and acknowledged my need for Him, He took a broken, desperate man and lifted him up so that he could tell others what the Lord Jesus Christ can do in their lives.

He did that for me!

But He let me go my own way first.

CHAPTER THREE

GETTING MY START
MY ROOTS IN ATHLETICS

had no idea that college football was in my future as my senior season at Rancocas Valley High School started in the fall of 1979. All I knew was that I loved the competition of high school football.

Since I was a little kid running around my neighborhood, I have loved sports—particularly football and baseball, as well as basketball. They were always a big part of my life when I was growing up. I started playing Little League baseball when I was seven years old, and about that same time I started playing football with my neighborhood friends.

Unlike a lot of kids who grow up playing sports, I wasn't what you would call a great sports "fan." I didn't hold up professional athletes as my heroes, although there were a few NFL players I looked up to. For example, I knew about the Steelers great Franco Harris because he played at my high school before going on to star at Penn State and later join the Pittsburgh Steelers, where he played on four Super Bowl championship teams. I also knew about a few of the other big-name players; guys like Fred Biletnikoff, Lynn Swann, Larry Csonka, Terry Bradshaw, and Mercury Morris.

I wasn't the kind of kid who had posters of professional athletes covering my bedroom walls. I didn't know anything about statistics, and I never looked up to those guys as my idols. Even in baseball, which was my favorite sport then, I would have been hard pressed to name some of the big stars in the game at the time.

I just liked to play.

My friends and I played sports outside for a couple of reasons—because we loved to play, and because that was all we had to do in our neighborhood. None of our parents could afford to buy us the kinds of toys that so many kids have now. We didn't have video games or roller blades or computers or VCRs. So to keep ourselves entertained, we got a ball and went out and played. When it was baseball season, we played baseball. During basketball season, we headed for the basketball court. During football season, it was football.

Although football has been both my ticket to college and the way I make my living, baseball has always been my first love. I started playing when I was seven and I guess you could say I was a natural at it. For some reason, I just knew how to run, catch, throw, and hit without anybody teaching me. I didn't start out playing T-ball, either. For me, it was real baseball from the very beginning—with pitchers, catchers, and the works.

As I got older, I moved up through the different levels of baseball—Little League, Babe Ruth, and so on—on through high school, where I had a good career as a pitcher and centerfielder for the Rancocas Valley High School team. I think I was a much better baseball player than football player, and I still think from time to time about what might have been if I'd pursued baseball after high school. About a year after I had committed to play football in college, I learned that the Philadelphia Phillies had scouted me at some of my high school games and had considered bringing me into their organization. I realize how greatly blessed I've been in my career in the National Football League, but it's still fun to wonder "what if" when I think about playing baseball. (I actually think I would have done quite well in professional baseball.)

While I played organized baseball from the time I started grade school, organized football didn't become a part of my life until my freshman year in high school. I didn't play Pop Warner football, and I didn't go out for the grade school or junior high school teams. But football was still a big part of my life.

My buddies and I used to play football in the streets of Mount Holly. Keeping our eyes open for oncoming cars, we'd play "rough touch" out in the streets of our neighborhood. "Rough touch" is actually something in between touch football and tackle. We tried not to get too rough on one another in the streets, but sometimes things would get a little out of hand, and we'd get scratched up pretty good. We'd run a play, then look to see if a car was coming before we ran another. When a car came, someone would yell, "Car!" and we'd move out of the way until the traffic cleared. Then we'd go back to playing.

Playing street football, and an occasional game of tackle when we could find a field to play in, gave me some helpful experience heading into my freshman year at Rancocas Valley. I played on the freshman team my first year, but from my sophomore season on, it was all varsity for me. By the time my junior and senior seasons rolled around, I had grown to about 5-10 1/2 and 180 pounds, and I was doing everything my team needed me to do. I played tight end and split end on offense and safety on our normal defense and linebacker on the goal-line defense. I also punted, placed-kicked, and returned kicks. During those last two seasons of high school football, I rarely came off the field.

I had a great time playing football then and I wish I could say that we had some great teams. But that's just not the way it happened. I played on high school teams during my junior and senior years at Rancocas Valley that, in all honesty, stunk. During my sophomore year, Giuseppe Harris, one of Franco Harris's younger brothers, played quarterback for us and led us deep into the state playoffs. But when Giuseppe and the rest of the seniors from that team graduated, they took with them any clue as to what it took to play winning football, and it was all downhill from there.

In spite of this, we had what I still think was the best talent in our league at the time. We had several guys on the team who were bigger, faster, and better football players than I was. The problem was that we were a bunch of head cases. We were uncoachable, unorganized, and just plain out of control. We had the talent to be as good as we wanted to be, but we just couldn't function as a team. We'd play fairly competitively in some of our games, but couldn't get the win.

The guys on the field those two seasons were a lot like me. In fact, all my buddies from G-Town were on the team, and we were representative of the other players who were on the team. We had so much junk in our lives that we couldn't come close to having the kind of self-discipline and sacrifice it takes to play winning football. Consequently, we significantly underachieved, finishing with records of 3-6 and 2-7 my junior and senior years.

Our coach, Bill Gordon, had a tough time dealing with us. One day during my senior year, he just blew up. We were in the midst of a tough season, and we'd been messing up pretty badly in practice and not concentrating on what we were doing that day. Finally, Coach Gordon had had enough. "That's it!" he yelled. "I quit! Forget you guys! Go ahead and do it yourselves!"

Bill Gordon was a good high school coach, and he'd been around for quite a while. He knew how to handle kids, but he was at a loss with this group. I can't say that I blame him for feeling like giving up on us.

He didn't totally give up on us, though. He stayed with the team and finished the season. He even took the time to sit down with several of us individually to have a little heart-to-heart. I still clearly remember what he said to me after one practice during my senior year. It wasn't long after an incident in which I'd gotten in a fight with one of my teammates. I'd been picked as a captain on the team, an honor I was nowhere near mature enough to handle. I told my teammate to do something and he wouldn't do it. Being the hothead that I was at the time, I jumped on him and started a fight. Obviously, that's not the kind of thing a football captain should be doing, but I felt like I needed to show this guy who was boss.

This wasn't the first time that I'd shown Coach Gordon what my temperament was really like. He wanted to make me his team's quarterback during my sophomore year, but knowing that the position requires a mature and levelheaded leader, he didn't do it because he realized I wasn't emotionally capable of handling it. I had all the athletic ability the position took, and Coach Gordon has since said that I would have made an excellent quarterback. The problem was that I was just too emotionally volatile and immature to handle the position.

When Coach Gordon found out about the fight with my teammate, he knew it was time for us to have a talk. He sat me down and told me in no uncertain terms that I was headed nowhere if I didn't rethink my approach to certain situations in life. "Irving, you could be something," Coach Gordon said. "But right now, you're just a hoodlum. If you don't change, you're never going to amount to anything."

Bill Gordon was a Christian man who cared about the kids he coached. He demonstrated his concern for me when I played for him at Rancocas Valley, and he continued to do that throughout my career at the University of Nebraska and in the National Football League. Even when I was going through the toughest times in my life—during the early years when I was playing for the New England Patriots—Coach Gordon did what he could to help make my situation better. I'd get a letter from him every now and then, and it would always come at the right time. I'd be feeling really low and over-whelmed by my situation, and I would find a letter of encouragement from Coach Gordon in my Sullivan Stadium mail box. It would usually say some-thing simple like, "I was just thinking about you and wanted to encourage you." When I look back on those letters, I'm grateful to Coach Gordon for taking the time to let me know he cared about me, that he hadn't given up on me. He didn't want anything, and he wasn't trying to preach at me to make me straighten out my life. He just wanted me to know that he cared about me. I still appreciate that.

But when we had our talk that day after practice, I didn't appreciate what he was saying. I was angry! I took what he was saying as a putdown, as a criti-cism of my effort on the football field. Coach Gordon said what he did to shock me, to get me to realize that if I didn't change my ways I was going nowhere—not to college and not into the Marines. He wasn't talking so much about my talent or effort as a football player as he was about my per-sonal life. He knew about the crowd I was hanging with and the things I was doing at night. He knew that I was getting into fights and looking for trouble. He even knew about the incident when I went through the plate glass win-dow at the pizza joint. Most of all, he knew the life I was leading had me headed nowhere quickly and that things could get a lot worse for me if I didn't straighten out.

Coach Gordon was right about my personal life, but hearing him tell me that I wasn't going to amount to anything made me angry. I didn't mind so much having him call me a hoodlum. It was the part about not amounting to anything that got to me. In my mind, what he was saying was a personal challenge to my effort.

I've always had motivation to be the best there was at anything I did. For example, I worked as a garbage collector a couple of summers when I was in high school. I worked with my brother-in-law, and I made $500-$600 a week, which was great money for a kid my age. I took pride in my work as a garbage man, and I worked hard because I wanted to be the best garbage man in Mount Holly. And I was, too. My brother-in-law and I would finish our routes before any of the other guys, and we'd end up going to help them finish. We took pride in getting the job done right and getting it done fast.

I worked a lot of jobs when I was in high school, and I approached all of them that way: I was going to be the best I could be in whatever it was I was doing. (Actually, this was true of my life as a hoodlum. As far as I was concerned, if I was going to be a hoodlum, I'd be the best hoodlum I could be.) It was that way when I played football, too. Even though our team was one of the worst in our league, I always wanted to be the best on the field in any given game. I worked hard on every play, and to have the coach tell me I would never amount to anything not only angered me, it motivated me. I felt like I had to show him that I *would* amount to something.

And I did. I exceeded even my own goals as a football player at Rancocas Valley High School that season, earning All-League, All-Burlington County, and All-American honors. It was through that effort that I started getting noticed as a college football prospect.

Getting a Look

With the postseason honors came something I didn't think would be coming my way—attention from some big-time college football recruiters. During my days in high school football it never even occurred to me that someone saw me as good enough to play at the major college level. But the coaches had seen something in me, and they started showing up after the season was over.

At first I was recruited by schools that, while they weren't major football powers, were located close to home. Rutgers (located in New Brunswick, New Jersey), Temple (Philadelphia), and a couple of others recruited me. Then bigger programs came calling—Nebraska, Pittsburgh, Penn State,

Southern California, Arizona, and Syracuse being among them. These were some pretty high-powered football programs, and I was surprised that they were interested in me. I had no idea that I had the kind of football talent it took to not only play Division I college football, but at some of the big-time schools that were recruiting me. Although I was All-League and All-County in high school and I had been named to an All-American team, I didn't know that any college programs were interested in me.

At that point, I still didn't know if college was for me. For one thing, I still wanted to fly jets. My plan was to join the United States Marine Corps and learn to fly. I could just see myself taking off and landing my F-15 on the deck of an aircraft carrier, and I was going to do whatever it took to realize that goal. I didn't know what it took to learn to fly jets, but I was determined to find out and then do it.

Mom, it turns out, had other plans.

Mother Knows Best

When the colleges started offering me scholarships to play football, my mother sat me down and told me that she wanted me to go to college and get an education. If I still wanted to go into the service and be a pilot after college, fine. Right now, though, if someone was going to give me money to pay my way through college, then I should do it. She pointed out to me that this wasn't just a free college education, but a chance for me to play more football.

Because I had a mom who took an interest in what I was doing, gave me some sense of limits, and wouldn't tolerate bad grades, as my senior year drew to a close, I had the grades and the clean record it took to have a chance to go to college and play football.

I listened to several college coaches give their pitches and explain to me why I should play for them, and I took five recruiting trips—to Maryland, Pittsburgh, Arizona, Temple, and Grambling. After a while, the whole thing started to get a little annoying. There were some coaches who came to my house and then dropped in on me at school. Some of them—I won't tell you which ones—promised my mom things like a house, trips, and other benefits.

Mom wasn't going to have any of that, though. We were going to do this honestly.

One of the programs that sent a recruiter to visit me was Penn State University's, coached by the legendary Joe Paterno. The coach who visited me seemed to think the Nittany Lions had a pretty good shot at me, and with good reason. At that time, anybody who was somebody from Rancocas Valley High School football went to Penn State to play college football. Franco Harris went there, followed by his brothers, Pete and Giuseppi. A couple of other Rancocas players followed as well. For a while, it seemed as if there was a pipeline between Mount Holly and University Park, Pennsylvania.

When the recruiter from Penn State came to my home, he acted as if my going to Penn State was a done deal, like he didn't even have to recruit me. He seemed to think that I'd go to Penn State just because those other players from Rancocas Valley had gone before me. It bothered me that they assumed that, and something inside me made me want to turn Penn State down. I wanted to make the decision on which college I would attend. I put a quick stop to it all when I made a simple announcement:

"I'm not going to go to Penn State."

Do You Wanna be a 'Husker?

Later that year, around mid-January, I got a call from a member of the University of Nebraska coaching staff asking me to come and visit the campus in Lincoln. They were interested in bringing me into their program as a defensive back. I knew Nebraska had one of the finest college football traditions in the land, and I figured if I went to a program like that I'd have a chance to play some by the time my senior year rolled around.

I took the trip to Nebraska, but it was the worst one I took that year. As far as I could tell, there was nothing for me in Lincoln. I got there on a Sunday during one of those Midwest snowstorms, and I spent almost the whole time in a hotel doing nothing. I had gone to some parties at the other schools and had a great time, but there was nothing going on for me here. I was bored out of my mind.

Tom Osborne, Nebraska's head coach, also made a trip of his own to my home. At first, I was uncomfortable about having him in my home because I was a little ashamed of it. It was an old house and kind of run down, and the furniture wasn't in very good condition. But Coach Osborne didn't care about that.

I don't know why, but there was something about Coach Osborne that really put me at ease as he just sat and talked with me as we ate pie and drank Kool-Aide that day in Mount Holly. It was that visit that got me thinking that Nebraska just might be the place for me after all.

One Final Choice

As it is for a lot of high school athletes, my decision on where to go to college was a tough one. I had several offers, and more than one of them looked pretty appealing.

One thing I had decided early in the process was that I'd be going to college wherever my friend Mike Rozier went. Mike, who would later go on to win the Heisman Trophy at Nebraska before moving on to play professional football, grew up in Camden, New Jersey, attending one of the schools I played against. Mike and I seemed to have a special connection with one another from the time we were kids. Our mothers grew up together and our fathers worked together. On top of that, he spent a lot of time at his grandmother's house, just two doors down from mine in Mount Holly. When Mike came to visit his grandmother in the summertime, we played football in the streets and hung out together. Soon, we became friends, and when we were seniors, we decided to go to the same college to play football.

It didn't take us long to narrow down our choices. It was between Pittsburgh and Nebraska. Finally, we decided on Coach Tom Osborne and the Cornhuskers.

Looking back on it, it's still hard for me to understand what was going through my mind when I decided to go to Nebraska. At the time, I was looking for something in a college, and Nebraska certainly didn't offer it. But I can also see that God somehow influenced my decision. Because He had a calling on my life, I think He knew that Nebraska was one place I could stay in class, stay on the football field, and stay out of trouble.

CHAPTER FOUR

HEADING FOR THE PLAINS
MY LIFE AS A CORNHUSKER

When I arrived at the University of Nebraska on August 13, 1980, the farthest thing from my mind was playing a key role on a Cornhusker team that would have a legitimate shot at winning the national championship.

I didn't think of myself as having that kind of talent. I figured I'd attend classes all four years, go to football practice and work hard, and maybe get to play a little bit by the time my senior year rolled around.

After that, I still had every intention of pursuing my goal of learning to fly. I had it all planned out. I was going to finish college, then take my diploma with me into the United States Marine Corps. I enrolled at Nebraska as a meteorology major, because I thought that would help me to get into pilot training after college.

But before I would have a chance to do anything after college, I was going to have to get through four years at the University of Nebraska, and that wouldn't happen unless I was able to endure what was going to be a tough freshman year for me.

A Homesick Freshman

It was tough for me to be so far away from home, especially in a place that was so different from what I had grown used to in Mount Holly. I might as well have been in a foreign country. Here I was, a young black man who had grown up in an all-black neighborhood in the city, now stuck out in the middle of nowhere with people who had no way of understanding my background or thinking (or I theirs). Everything I did and said was different from what the people around me were doing and saying. I mean no disrespect to the people at the University of Nebraska. They were really good to me, and I still appreciate that. But being so far away from my home and my neighborhood was a major culture shock.

What made things worse for me was that I didn't know the city of Lincoln and didn't have a car or any way to get around. I had to walk everywhere, and that limited where I could go. My roommate, Turner Gill, a freshman who had come to Nebraska as a quarterback, had a car so he was gone most of the time. More often than not, I was stuck in my dorm room by myself, with nobody to talk to and nothing to do.

The hardest part of that year was that my friend Mike Rozier wouldn't be joining me. He was in Coffeyville, Kansas, attending Coffeyville Junior College to work on his grades before coming to Nebraska for his sophomore year. We'd decided together that we were coming to Nebraska, and I knew coming into my freshman year that he wouldn't be there. I couldn't wait for Mike to join me for our sophomore season.

I couldn't shake my homesickness, my loneliness, my boredom, and my feelings of isolation. All I could think about was how miserable I was away from my friends. Almost from the time I arrived in Lincoln, I wanted to go home. I'd call home a lot and talk to my mom and sisters. Sometimes they'd get on different phone lines and sing what I called "church songs" to me. It was comforting to talk to them, but it also made me want to go home even more. I wanted out of Lincoln.

I stuck it out that first term in school, and I did have a good time playing some college football that first year.

Freshman Football

While Mike Rozier was playing football and bringing up his grades at Coffeyville Junior College, I was busy playing on the freshman football team at Nebraska. I had been recruited by Nebraska as a defensive back, but I was moved to the flanker position on offense the day I arrived and stayed at that position all four years.

Our freshman team had a great 1980 season. Turner Gill and I were the main men on the team, and we won all six of our games big with an average of sixty-three points a game. We played other schools' junior varsity teams and we still blew them out. I enjoyed playing freshman football, despite the fact that it was a short season.

The end of freshman football wasn't the end of the season for me. Turner and I were both brought up to the varsity team for the final third of the season and the Cornhuskers' 31-17 win over Mississippi State in the Sun Bowl in El Paso, Texas. Coach Osborne was well known for his steadfast refusal to play true freshmen on the varsity, but he must have seen something in Turner and me (or, at least, heard something), as we were not only brought up from the freshman team that year, but given some playing time. We both were sent into a couple of blowout games to mop up, and we even had a hand in scoring a few touchdowns.

It was a big honor to me to be brought up to the varsity team my freshman year, joining Dave Rimington, Roger Craig, Jarvis Redwine, Andra Franklin, Jeff Quinn, and the rest of the team. It was also exciting to have a chance to dress for the Sun Bowl.

The sense of excitement I felt over getting promoted to varsity didn't overcome my sense of wanting out of Nebraska. So, the first time I went home for a holiday break, I had an announcement for my parents and the Nebraska coaches—I wasn't going back.

Going (Staying?) Home

I had made up my mind that there was no way I was going back to Nebraska, and nobody was going to change it. I just didn't like it there. It wasn't home, and it wasn't the kind of place I was used to. I decided when I first got there that I would finish out that first term, knowing that I'd have a chance to go home after that. And when I went home, I intended to stay there.

My announcement that I wasn't going back to college didn't sit well with Mom or Dad, although Dad was more prone to letting me make my own decision. The three of us argued about it the whole time I was home. When it was time for me to go to the airport, my bags still weren't packed because I had no intention of going back. Mom, tired of trying to talk me into going back to school, turned to Dad for some support.

"David, tell Irving he's got to go back to school!" she pleaded, hoping Dad would force me to get in the car with him so he could take me to the airport.

"Look," Dad said, "he's grown! He can make his own decision."

Then, turning his attention on me, Dad said, "Are you going back or not? I've got to go to work, so make up your mind right now!"

I said, "I ain't going."

With that settled—at least as far as I was concerned at the time—Dad left and went to work. I stayed home.

Eventually, though, after I was a week late getting back to school, one of the Nebraska coaches called me and somehow persuaded me to come back. I don't remember what he said, but it must have been good, because prior to that I had no intention of even thinking about going back to Lincoln.

After returning, things did get better for me. I survived what to that point had been the toughest year in my life. Things really got better for me as I headed into my sophomore year.

Getting Used to Lincoln

My sophomore year was better than my freshman year from the start for the simple reason that I had gotten to know some people and made some friends. It also helped that I had a car and was able to get around a little more.

It also helped that Mike Rozier was there. He'd successfully finished his year at Coffeyville Junior College, and now it was time for us to play college football together.

I was pleasantly surprised as a sophomore to find that I would be playing regularly on the Cornhusker varsity. I alternated with Anthony Steels at flanker and ran plays in for the offense. I was our punt returner, and I finished first in the conference and fourth in the nation in punt returning that season. (Mike Rozier returned kickoffs, too, but you don't get a lot of kickoff returns when you play for Nebraska.) Mike was a sophomore sensation for the Huskers, rushing for 943 yards as he teamed in the backfield with half-back Roger Craig, fullback Phil Bates, and Turner Gill at quarterback as we finished 9-3.

I started to come into my own as a player that year as well. At the beginning of my sophomore year, I still didn't know if I had the ability to play at the level I needed to succeed in a program like Nebraska's. I got a boost in confidence during our second game of the season against Florida State. The Seminoles' punter, Rohn Stark, got off a beauty of a kick that sailed about seventy yards. I fielded the kick at our 18-yard line, and eighty-two yards later, I had my first collegiate touchdown. We beat FSU 34-14. I was happy that the team won, but I was ecstatic to realize that I belonged on the Nebraska football team. From then on, things seemed to take off for me.

Mike Rozier, Turner Gill, and I went on to have a great three-year run with the Cornhuskers, a run in which we accomplished some great things in college football, but in which we were unable to accomplish one goal we had set for ourselves.

Falling Short of #1

I was never part of a national championship team at Nebraska, but my teammates and I got close to the national title all three years I played on the varsity team. Each year—1981, 1982, and 1983—we lost to the team that went on to get voted the best Division I college football team in the nation. All three years, we won the Big-8 championship (we were 21-0 in conference play over those three seasons) but lost a key non-conference or bowl game to miss out on the national title.

My sophomore year, we finished 7-0 in the conference and earned the right to play 11-0 Clemson in the Orange Bowl. The Tigers beat us 22-17 and won the national championship, while we finished eleventh in the final Associated Press poll that year.

We had a great team at Nebraska my junior year. We again won the Big-8 championship and again earned a spot in the Orange Bowl, this time against Louisiana State. We won a 21-20 thriller as Mike Rozier rushed for 118 yards and Turner Gill passed for 184. I had a huge game, racking up eighty-four yards on five catches, twelve yards rushing, and another fifty-six yards on two punt returns.

The only thing that stood between us and the national championship was our 27-24 loss to eventual champion Penn State in a non-conference game the second week of the season in State College, Pennsylvania. The Lions got a gift that day. We knew it, they knew it, and the rest of the world knew it. Penn State won the game with a touchdown with just seconds left in the game, but the Lions were helped when their tight end, Mike McCloskey was given a reception at their two-yard line when he was out of bounds. All the replays showed that he was out of bounds, but he was given the catch. On the next play, they scored on a touchdown pass with four seconds left. The Lions won.

We were 11-1 that year, good for second in the polls. Penn State won the national championship. All that year, I had people asking me about "the Call" that gave the Nittany Lions the help they needed to beat us that day. I couldn't wait for a chance to get some payback for that game, and we got it during my senior year with a 44-6 blowout in the season-opening Kickoff Classic in East Rutherford, New Jersey.

As tough as it is still for me to think about how close we came to winning the national championship my junior year, the disappointment of that loss is nothing compared with what happened to us my senior year.

The Best Team Ever?

With almost all our key players back from the 1982 season, we were the favorites at the outset of the '83 campaign to win the national title. From day one, we were ranked number one in the nation, and we didn't let up during the regular season, going 11-0 and earning a spot in the Orange Bowl.

We weren't just winning our games, either. We were tearing people apart with a devastating offense that featured first-team All-American halfback Mike Rozier (also the Heisman Trophy winner), offensive lineman Dean Steinkuhler (the Outland Trophy and Lombardi Award winner), and me at flanker, not to mention an outstanding all-purpose quarterback in Turner Gill.

People still say that the 1983 Nebraska offense may have been the best ever in college football. The writers were comparing us with the best that ever played, saying that we were as good or better than they had been. One look at the numbers tells the story. We averaged 545 yards a game in total offense, led the nation in rushing with more than 400 yards a game, and scored almost fifty-seven points a game during the regular season. We were led by Rozier's 2,148 yards rushing, 2,486 all-purpose yards (receiving, rushing, and return yards combined), and twenty-nine touchdowns. Turner passed for more than 1,500 yards and threw for fourteen touchdowns that year—not bad for an option quarterback—and I had 780 yards and eight touchdowns receiving and 1,267 all-purpose yards.

For the most part, we just had our way on the football field. We scored almost at will, racking up more than forty points nine times and more than fifty points seven times. We scored more than sixty points five times and twice went over the seventy-point mark. Our season high? Eighty-four in our game with the University of Minnesota in Minneapolis. Only two of our games—our 14-10 win over Oklahoma State and our 28-21 victory over Oklahoma—were close.

As the Big-8 champions and as the top-ranked team in the nation, we earned the chance to play for the national championship against the Miami Hurricanes in the Orange Bowl.

Miami was on a roll of its own coming into the Orange Bowl, having won ten in a row after a 28-3 season-opening loss to Florida. The Hurricanes had climbed to fourth in the Associated Press by the time the regular season ended. They had some great players, including quarterback Bernie Kosar, who, as a red-shirt freshman that season, threw for more than 2,300 yards. They also had tight end Glenn Dennison, wide receiver Eddie Brown, running back Albert Bentley, and linebackers Jay Brophy, Ken Sisk, and Jack Fernandez.

Miami also had added motivation, as it was to be Howard Schnellenberger's last as coach of the Hurricanes. Schnellenberger had become something of a hero in south Florida, having taken a Miami program that was in shambles—eight losing seasons out of the ten prior to his arrival in 1979—and given it not just respectability, but national prominence.

Even though the rest of the nation was saying that we were unbeatable and that there was no way these mere mortals from Miami could even stay on the field with us, Coach Schnellenberger had his team believing that they could not only compete with us, but beat us. And he had his Hurricanes ready to do anything he asked of them in order to achieve that goal.

Miami had a tough defense that was fourth in the nation in yardage and third in points allowed that year—the Hurricanes gave up less than ten points a game—but people pointed out that it was no match in size for our offense. Our front line outweighed theirs by an *average* of more than thirty-five pounds per man. Most people thought we'd just overpower them the way we had everybody else that season. We were eleven-point favorites, but a lot of folks thought that was a pretty conservative point spread.

On paper, it looked like we'd roll over the Hurricanes and into the national championship. But, as the old saying goes, games aren't played on paper. So, on January 2, 1984, the University of Miami pulled one of the biggest college football upsets of all time in one of the greatest college football games ever played.

The Hurricanes came out and jumped all over us that night. Before we knew what hit us, we were down 17-0 after Kosar threw two touchdown passes to Dennison and Jeff Davis kicked a field goal.

The Miami defense—that same Miami defense that most people thought we would shove around the field all game long—pretty much put the clamps on our running game in the first half. We moved the ball, but they were stopping us from breaking big plays, a trademark of the Cornhusker offense. We were shut out in the first quarter, and it took a trick play to finally get us in the end zone. It was what people called a "Fumblerooski," and it called for Turner Gill to deliberately put the ball on the ground so that offensive guard Dean Steinkuhler could scoop it up and run with it. It worked to perfection as Dean picked up the ball and rumbled nineteen yards to make it 17-7.

Turner scored on a sneak late in the first half, and we kicked a field goal early in the third quarter to tie it. At that point, it seemed like we had the momentum. A lot of people—probably us included—thought we would take over from there and blow the Hurricanes off the field.

But a funny thing happened on the way to our second-half explosion. The explosion didn't happen.

Miami came back with two scores—one on a seventy-five-yard drive for a touchdown by freshman fullback Alonzo Highsmith and the other on an Albert Bentley run—to take a 31-17 lead with less than twelve minutes left. At that point, it looked like there would be a blowout, but it was we who were getting blown out.

We still had an offense that could score quickly from anywhere on the field, and once again, we came from behind. We drove seventy-six yards, and Jeff Smith, who came in for Rozier when Mike twisted a left ankle in the third quarter, scored on a one-yard run to make it 31-24. We got the ball back for one last shot after Miami missed a field goal attempt with one minute, forty-seven seconds left in the game. The problem was we were seventy-four yards away from the goal line.

Led by Turner Gill, we drove right down the field, and were quickly in position to score when I had the most embarrassing—and, unfortunately, one of the most memorable—moments I've ever had on a football field. I was running a route down the middle and I got open in the end zone when Turner Gill threw me the ball. I might have relaxed a little too much or I might have gotten bumped by a defensive back, I don't remember, but I was open when the ball got there. But I didn't make the catch. As the ball came in, I put up my hands to catch it, but I had my hands too far apart, and the point of the ball hit my hip pad, and I dropped it.

Right there, on national television, in the biggest college football game of the year—of my career—I dropped an easy pass. I had no excuses. It should have been a touchdown. It was a very catchable ball, but I just dropped it. That was the only pass I dropped that whole year, and it happened to be in the national championship game. I was devastated. All I could hope for was a chance to redeem myself.

That chance never came for me personally, but it did for my team. With less than a minute left in the game, Smith took a pitch from Turner Gill on a fourth-down play and ran twenty-four yards for a touchdown to make it 31-30. Now, it was decision time.

Coach Osborne hardly hesitated, sending in our two-point conversion team to go for the win. As it turns out, we would have won the national championship with a tie, and we had a dependable kicker. But our coaches didn't see it that way. They wanted to go for the win. They didn't want to "back into" a national title.

Coach Schnellenberger sent in Miami's two-point conversion defense— the goal-line defense—before our two-point conversion team was even on the field. He seemed to know what our coaches were thinking.

Now, it was time. This was for all the marbles. If we scored, we were the champs. If we didn't, Miami would get the crown.

Turner Gill took the snap, rolled right, and threw. But Kenny Calhoun, Miami's defensive back, got his finger tips on the ball, which was a little behind Jeff Smith but might still have been catchable.

The ball fell harmlessly to the ground.

We fell from the top spot in the polls.

Thousands of Orange Bowl fans poured onto the field to celebrate the biggest win in the history of Miami Hurricane football. The Miami players jumped around, embraced each other with tears of joy running down their faces, and led the home crowd in the frenzied celebration.

We were in shock. This wasn't supposed to be happening. It *couldn't* be happening. That night was supposed to be the final touch on a perfect season, a national championship season. It's hard for me to remember what I was doing as I saw the Orange Bowl field turn into a celebration for the other team. I'm pretty sure I was shedding some tears. I'd lost the goat horns when we scored that last touchdown, but it still hurt to lose that chance to be the best in the nation. I'd always strived to be the best at whatever it was I was doing, and I wanted that national championship. I almost couldn't believe what had just happened to us. I barely slept that night. In fact, I lost quite a bit of sleep over the weeks and months that followed.

Miami's win, which broke a Nebraska winning streak of twenty-two games over two seasons, combined with Georgia's 10-9 win over previously unbeaten Texas in the Cotton Bowl, gave the Hurricanes the national championship. The next day, Miami was voted number one in both the Associated Press and the United Press International polls. We were second in both.

Living with a Loss

I still feel a sense of disappointment when I think about that night in Miami. We were so close to being named the best team in college football, only to fall one pass short of the Orange Bowl win and the national championship.

I'm still grateful that God guided my footsteps to Nebraska and that He gave me coaches who persuaded me to stay there when, if it had been totally up to me, I would have bolted before my freshman year was even half finished.

Looking back on my days in Lincoln, I can plainly see that God guided me there, sustained me when I wanted to leave, and kept me out of trouble. With hindsight, I can see that if I'd gone to the University of Southern California or some other school in a large metropolitan area, I probably would have gotten myself in the kind of trouble that would have gotten me kicked out of school—or worse. In Lincoln, there just wasn't much to do.

God guided me even though I still hadn't acknowledged my calling to preach. I still didn't know Jesus Christ as my Savior. I remembered who He was, and I even prayed from time to time. But as far as being committed to Him and His will for me, I wasn't even close.

Although it was my worst recruiting trip, and I was bored out of my mind when I visited Lincoln and was depressed at the thought of living there, something inside said, "Go to Nebraska!"

I'm also grateful to God for allowing me to play football at Nebraska, to have the chance to accomplish great things on the football field with my friends on that team and the chance to play for the national championship, not once but twice. Finally, I'm grateful to have played for a man who did more to shape my life than I could have understood at the time, Tom Osborne.

A Coaching Legend

Tom Osborne isn't just somebody I look back on as a great football coach. To me, he was also a great teacher and a great example of standing for something positive.

I didn't realize when I first went to Nebraska that Coach Osborne was a

Christian man. In fact, I didn't think it was possible for someone to be involved in football at that level and be a Christian. To me, it didn't look like there were many people involved in the game—players or coaches—who weren't cussing and carrying on like everybody else. I didn't know many players or coaches who professed to be Christians, at least not so everybody could hear it.

But as I got to know Tom and observed the way he carried himself, I saw there was something different in him. He didn't preach at us or try to convert us, but there was something about him that set him apart from the other people I knew. I still remember the first time somebody told me he was a strong Christian man. I thought, *That's right, he doesn't cuss.*

Coach Osborne had an influence on my life that has lasted to this day. That influence didn't come from him preaching at me, but in the way he carried himself, his demeanor, and what he stood for. He never wavered to the right or to the left, but was consistent in all his ways. If he said something, we could count on it.

Because Tom carried himself that way in front of us, we were that way as a team. I didn't understand it at the time, but now I look back and can see it. Without even thinking about it, we carried ourselves with the confidence and conviction that Tom Osborne had imparted to us.

I know that a lot of folks might look at Tom and say, "He says he's a Christian, but look at some of the things his players have done." I'd be the first to admit that some players from the University of Nebraska football program have done some less-than-admirable things in recent years. All that stuff is on the public record and can't be hidden. But I'd also be the first to stand up for Tom Osborne and say that it's not fair to blame him for these things. Coach Osborne has always been very concerned about how his players conduct themselves on and off the football field, but at the same time, he can't hold their hands twenty-four hours a day. Each young man who goes to the Nebraska football program—or any program for that matter—must make his own decisions.

Coach Osborne, whose program was once considered a model for other football programs, was severely criticized a few years back over his handling of the situation with running back Lawrence Phillips, who now plays for the St. Louis Rams. Phillips had been charged with assault in connection with an incident with a former girlfriend. He was suspended from the team but was later reinstated.

People criticized Tom and said all he cared about was winning football games and that it didn't matter to him if one of the players who helped him win was guilty of abusing his former girlfriend. The criticism came from all corners of society, and it didn't let up.

As someone who has known Tom Osborne for years, I know those criticisms are wrong. Coach Osborne fully realized the seriousness of Phillips's actions, and he in no way condoned or excused them. But, as a Christian man, a praying man, Coach Osborne believed in giving a person a second chance. As far as I'm concerned, Tom did what was right, and that was to forgive and let that player have a second chance. The player had done something no one should get away with. But he also was punished for what he did. Tom Osborne said from the beginning that he would bring the player back after all that was done, and when it was time to bring him back, Tom stood by what he said. That's what Jesus would have done, and that's what Tom did.

Coach Osborne planted a seed in me through the way he lived and through the way he talked. That seed would one day sprout in my life, but not before I went through some tough times.

Those tough times, it turns out, got started early, even before I left the University of Nebraska.

Problems and Rumors of Problems

It was just before the 1984 National Football League draft when I first heard about the rumor: Someone said that I intentionally dropped that pass in the 1984 Orange Bowl which would have put us in position to win or tie the game. I was accused of attempting to throw the game, and it was rumored that I had been "paid off" to help Miami win.

I couldn't believe what I was hearing! It made me sick inside to think that someone could believe that about me. I was still kicking myself for that drop and blaming myself for our loss of the national championship that night in Miami. (Remember, we ended up scoring a few plays later, so that drop really didn't affect the outcome.) I never would have even thought about throwing a game, and now someone was saying that I'd dropped the pass intentionally.

To this day, I still have no idea where the rumor was started or by whom. I don't know if it was started by somebody who had lost money on the game or if it was started by some off-the-cuff comment. It might have been some disappointed Nebraska fan. I do know that I did not drop the pass intentionally. I was doing everything I could to help my team win the 1984 Orange Bowl and the national championship. I've made some mistakes in my past, but I wouldn't—and didn't—intentionally drop that pass.

Unfortunately people still remember the drop and the accusations. To this day, I still have people asking me about it.

But that wasn't the only problem I had to deal with before I went into the NFL. Later that year, just before I was to leave Lincoln, I was accused of beating up a young woman I had formerly dated. The accusations that I punched her came after I had gone to her apartment to retrieve a chair I had left there. Again, it didn't happen the way it was portrayed in the press. There was a physical confrontation involved, but I never hit her.

Being the hothead I was, I had kicked in her door to get the chair. As I was carrying it to my car, there was a physical confrontation between us, but one that she started. All I did was restrain her so that she wouldn't beat on me or my car. But she told the police that I'd hit her, and when those kinds of accusations are made, they stick, even if they aren't true. I still get asked about that incident, even though it was well over a decade ago. But the truth, the whole truth, is that I never hit the woman. I had a quick temper, but I never hit her. I was doing everything I could to keep from *being* hit.

While some things happened at the end of my senior year at Nebraska that I thought weren't fair to me, it really seems that they were just the beginning of the trouble I would find myself getting into once I started my career in the National Football League.

CHAPTER FIVE

FOOTBALL AS MY VOCATION

ON TO THE NFL

As hard as it may be for some people to believe, playing professional football wasn't something I gave a lot of thought to when I was in college. As I mentioned before, my plan was to join the United States Marine Corps after graduation and learn to fly jets.

That all changed during my senior year, a season in which I was named a consensus All-American and touted as one of the Cornhuskers' three Heisman Trophy candidates. (The other two were Mike Rozier and Turner Gill. Mike ended up winning the award, and rightly so, as he led the nation in rushing and in points scored.)

As the season wore on, the Cornhuskers kept hearing that we could be the best college football team of all time, that we were a lock for an unde-feated season and the national championship.

By now, everybody knows what happened to our title aspirations. The good news for me, Mike Rozier, and offensive lineman Dean Steinkuhler (among others) is that we were getting plenty of attention from the pro scouts. It looked like several of us from that team would be playing profes-sional football in the National Football League (or the now-defunct United States Football League).

Early that year, I was still pretty oblivious to what was happening to me. I was still naive Irving from Mount Holly, and I didn't yet realize that I was good enough to play professional football. But as the year wore on, I started hearing how I was not only a pro football prospect, but a potential first-round draft pick.

Making Comparisons

All through my senior year I heard and read about people comparing me to former Husker great Johnny Rodgers. The biggest difference between me and Johnny—other than the fact that I was bigger—was that I didn't dominate the offense the way he did. I touched the ball an average of about four times a game, partly because we had so many offensive weapons and partly because the starters didn't usually play much because we were blowing people out. Playing on a team that had the kind of national exposure and that played the kind of offense it did allowed me to show the pro scouts what I could do, even if I didn't get to do it that often.

I didn't mind not touching the ball that much in college. I actually think it helped me in the long run. I've never been the kind of football player who had to dominate or be the "main man" on my team, so in college I did whatever was asked of me to help the team. I ran my routes, I caught the ball, I returned kicks, I ran, I blocked. When I didn't have the ball, I blocked for Mike, or Turner, or anyone else who had the ball. And I loved it. I liked the contact, and I liked doing things to help my teammates do well on the football field. Doing all that blocking gave the pro scouts a picture that I wanted them to see: that I was a complete football player, and not just a good receiver.

That approach to the game paid off for me as I was projected as one of the top picks of the draft. The scouts saw me as a versatile player who could do it all—run, block, catch, and return kicks. Some of them even conjectured that I had the strength, speed, and size to make a good NFL running back.

Getting Drafted

Heading into the 1984 draft, the word around the NFL was that I was going to be the first overall pick by the Cincinnati Bengals. Mike Rozier, who could have been the top pick that year, signed with the United States Football League's Pittsburgh Maulers that January. That left me for the Bengals.

The problem was, I didn't want to go to Cincinnati. I told the Bengals that much over the phone. So, instead of drafting me and wasting the top pick in the draft when I went to the USFL (I had been looking into going to the USFL, but hadn't worked out any contract at that time), the Bengals worked out a deal with the Houston Oilers, who had the second pick in the draft, to allow the Oilers to take me.

I was excited at the thought of playing for the Oilers. Sure, they'd gone through a horrible stretch during the few years leading to the 1984 draft—2-14 in 1983—but they were in the process of rebuilding, having signed Warren Moon out of the Canadian Football League, where he became the only quarterback in the history of professional football to pass for 5,000 yards two seasons in a row. Granted, that wasn't in the NFL, but those were still amazing numbers. I talked to Warren over the phone about going to Houston, and I was convinced Houston was the place for me.

But it never happened.

I was all set to go to the Oilers, but a major pre-draft trade on April 5 changed my plans. The New England Patriots traded their two first-round picks—sixteenth and twenty-eighth—and a couple of other lower picks to the Bengals for the first pick in the draft. The Patriots already had a good crew of receivers, including Stanley Morgan, but they said from the outset that their intention was to take me with that first pick.

I was at the Draft Day proceedings on May 1, 1984, at the Omni Park Central Hotel in New York City, but the announcement that I was the first pick in the May 1-2 draft was a mere formality. I had already signed my first National Football League contract and got ready to head to Massachusetts.

Rookie Year Struggles

The New England Patriots appeared to be on their way up when I joined the team for training camp in the summer of 1984. They hadn't won a division championship since 1978 and they had fallen to 2-14 in 1981, but they had the talent, the balance, and the depth to be a factor in the American Football Conference's Eastern Division. Most observers felt they were on the verge of big things in the NFL.

We had a good, fast crew of receivers (Morgan, Stephen Starring, Cedric Jones, Darryal Wilson, and Clarence Weathers), a solid offensive line, a strong running game, and a defense with some potential. At quarterback we had Steve Grogan, with Tony Eason, the team's top draft pick of 1983, waiting in the wings.

We got off to a fast start, going 5-2 after a win over the Bengals in week seven. We looked like a lock for the playoffs after that win. But something was missing. After a 44-24 loss to Miami—our second blowout loss to the Dolphins in as many games—our AFC East rivals and the eventual division champions, Coach Ron Meyer, who had the reputation as having a tough time relating to the players at the professional level, was fired and replaced with Raymond Berry, the Hall of Fame receiver who had played for the Baltimore Colts.

We were 5-3 after our loss to the Dolphins and still in the thick of the playoff chase. But when Coach Berry came in, he took his time implementing his own system, a move a lot of people thought was a mistake. We struggled the rest of the season, closing out 4-4 over the second half of the year to finish with a 9-7 non-playoff season record.

The season was somewhat frustrating for me personally, as I struggled with some injuries—a rib injury in the preseason and a dislocated shoulder against Miami in the regular season. These injuries caused me to miss two games and kept me on the bench for most of the others. I had only eleven receptions and one touchdown catch for the season, hardly the kind of numbers you'd expect from the top pick in the draft. On the plus side, I finished fourth in the AFC and sixth in the NFL in punt return average. But more was expected of me. Much more.

While the New England Patriots came nowhere near to living up to their potential in 1984, there was reason for optimism going into 1985. We still had a talented group of football players, and they would be starting the season with Coach Berry.

Before I had a chance to enjoy my second year in the National Football League, I went through an off-season that would see me taking a life-changing step.

It was time for me to get married.

Meeting Jacqui

I met my wife, Jacqueline Cooper, through Katherine Kennedy, a woman who was working for Patriots General Manager Pat Sullivan. I'd talked to Katherine from time to time during my rookie year, and one day I told her how lonely I was and how hard a time I had getting around the Boston area. All I knew was how to get from my home to Sullivan Stadium. I asked her if she knew anybody who could show me around and keep me company. So Katherine set me up on a blind date with Jacqui, who was her goddaughter.

Our first date was October 1. I looked forward to meeting her, but I have to be honest and say that our first date didn't go as well as I had hoped. We argued quite a bit, and it just didn't seem like we had much in common. After that evening, I decided not to call her again. I really didn't want to go out again, and I didn't think it would be a big deal for her, either.

I was wrong on that point.

Jacqui was pretty ticked off at me for not calling her back, and she was looking for a chance to tell me that much. One game day that November, she come to one of my games at Sullivan Stadium to tell me off. When I saw her, though, I had my own change of heart. To me, she didn't look like the same person I had dated the month before. She was decked out in these beautiful leather pants, and she looked great! (She was a cheerleader for the USFL's Boston Breakers, so you know she had something going for her, looks-wise.)

So instead of getting told off, I set up another date with Jacqui. We went out again, and soon we were going out steadily. Not long after that, I asked her to marry me.

Until then, I'd been to a lot of places and met a lot of people, including a lot of women. But Jacqui was different than anyone I'd ever met. At that point, it didn't matter to me if I was ready to get married. I had found somebody that I knew I wanted to hang on to and keep in my life. We were married by a justice of the peace in Brockton, Massachusetts, on January 11, 1985, after my first season with the Patriots ended.

While I usually recommend that a person spend more time with someone before marrying than Jacqui and I did, I can look back and see that God brought her into my life at just the right time.

When my rookie season ended in New England, I was nowhere near ready to get married—emotionally or spiritually. It was right around this time that I started living hard and fast. I'd started hanging out with some guys on the Patriots who introduced me to what we thought was the "good life" of a professional athlete. Soon I was drinking, using drugs, and hanging out in the clubs.

Jacqueline and I had no idea what being a husband and a wife was all about when we got married, and we went through some rough times in our relationship during the first six years together. We were both young kids still trying to figure things out, and being together only complicated some things in our lives.

I can see that God was looking out for me, because I've realized that getting married at that time had a stabilizing effect on my life. I believe that if I hadn't gotten married when I did, my life would have become even more of a mess than it eventually did. Being married gave me a sense of not going too far, even though I was doing some things that I knew were wrong and we had a lot of problems. It put some sense of limits on my life.

I needed that sense of limits as I moved on in my career with the New England Patriots.

A Super Bowl Season

The 1985 New England Patriots were one of those "Rocky Balboa" stories that come along every so often in sports. While we had as much talent as any team in the American Football Conference, we took the long route to Super Bowl XX, fighting through three road playoff games to make it to the biggest football game of the year.

We had our share of quality football players that season. Tony Eason had come into his own in 1984, passing for more than 3,000 yards. Stanley Morgan, Stephen Starring, and I were considered the fastest group of receivers in the NFL. As a group, our running backs were among the best in the league. Craig James, who came to the Patriots after being cut by a USFL team, and Tony Collins were our halfbacks. Our offensive line was led by Pro Bowlers John Hannah at left guard and Brian Holloway at left tackle. Andre

Tippett, an outside linebacker who had established himself as one of the best pass rushers in the game, led our defense.

Managing all that talent was Raymond Berry, a man I came to respect and love, not just as a coach but as a human being. Raymond was a player's coach, someone we could all relate to, and, I'm almost embarrassed to say now, someone I'd never heard of before he came to New England.

Before Raymond came to coach us, I didn't know that he was one of the greatest receivers to ever play the game and that he left the NFL as the league's all-time leading receiver at the time. I also didn't know that he was a hero in Baltimore, where he and Johnny Unitas teamed as one of the greatest quarterback-receiver tandems in league history, nor that Raymond was in the Hall of Fame and had been since his induction in 1973.

I learned that Raymond Berry was a great player because of what people told me after he got to New England. I found out on my own—as did my teammates—that he was also a great coach. I think he was great because he knew what it took to play well and win. He also knew what football players put their bodies and minds through, and he built his program around what he knew. For example, he understood that players over thirty would often need an extra day off to let their bodies recover from the previous game, so he'd give them the day off practice.

Raymond Berry earned our respect because he had a way of letting us know where we stood with him and what he expected from us. He was also the kind of coach who knew how important it was for us to prepare ourselves.

Raymond Berry once said, "Luck is what happens when preparation meets opportunity." He was an example of that. As a player, he had the reputation as being almost obsessive about running perfect routes and with making sure he was ready for any game situation. As a player in the fifties and sixties, Berry spent hours of extra time before and after practice just catching the ball. He'd catch up to—and probably more than—a hundred balls a day. He'd catch them from all angles and at all heights. He'd catch them falling down or jumping. If there was a way to catch a football, Raymond Berry practiced it.

And he made us do the same.

Coach Berry would make us catch 150 balls a day. If you weren't running a play at one of Coach Berry's practices, then you'd better be somewhere catching a football. And not just straight-on catches with your hands out in front of you, but diving catches, one-handed catches, catches with the tips of your toes on the sideline, and catches with somebody bumping you.

Everybody had to practice catching and hanging onto footballs—even the offensive linemen. What looked like an obsession during practice later became just another part of preparation for our run in the playoffs. It seemed like there was an instance in every playoff game that year when someone who wasn't used to carrying the ball, a place-kick holder or an offensive guard, for example, had to handle the ball during a game because of a fumble or an interception.

Some of the things Coach Berry had us do in practice might have seemed silly to some of us, but it was his attention to detail, his commitment to making us the best we could be, that took us on that amazing run through the playoffs and into Super Bowl XX.

The Road Warriors

The 1985 New England Patriots captured the imagination of sports fans across the country by doing what seemed impossible: going from a wild card playoff position, winning three playoff games on the road, and moving on to play in the Super Bowl.

We finished the regular season with an 11-5 record, good for a second-place tie with the New York Jets in the AFC Eastern Division. Both New England and the New York Jets took the wild card spots, edging out 11-5 Denver on the tie-breakers. Miami won the division with a 12-4 record.

We were a historically weak road team, so it wouldn't have surprised anyone if we'd just faded away early in the playoffs. But it didn't happen. Instead, each week we established ourselves as the NFL's true "Road Warriors" of the 1985 playoffs.

Our run through the playoffs started at Giants Stadium in East Rutherford, New Jersey, in a December 28 game against the New York Jets in the AFC East wild card game. We won 26-14 as Tony Franklin provided the margin of victory with an NFL playoff-tying record four field goals.

We then traveled to Los Angeles to meet the Raiders in a divisional playoff game at Memorial Coliseum. We were down 17-7 before rallying for the 27-20 win and a date with the Miami Dolphins at the Orange Bowl for the American Football Conference championship.

While a lot of people were impressed by the run we'd made in the playoffs heading into the AFC championship game, most thought it would be all over that week. The writers were pointing out how the Patriots had won only twice before in Miami and how they'd lost nineteen straight there. But the New England faithful remained optimistic. Homes, restaurants, and other businesses in the Boston area sported signs that read "Squish the Fish."

"Squish the Fish" is exactly what we did, winning 31-14 and setting up our Super Bowl appearance against the Chicago Bears at the New Orleans Superdome.

This was the Patriots' finest moment. After twenty-six years of floundering around in mediocrity, the Pats were in the biggest game of the 1985 season. Although they didn't get to see us in a home playoff game that year, our fans were going crazy with Super Bowl Fever.

But our finest moment turned quickly to embarrassment on Super Bowl Sunday, as we were destroyed by the Bears 46-10 in front of 127 million television viewers in the most lopsided Super Bowl in the history of the game.

Super Bowl Humiliation

We were a good team, but the Bears were a great team. Featuring players like Walter Payton, Mike Singletary, Richard Dent, Jim McMahon, Willie Gault, William "the Refrigerator" Perry, and Steve McMichael, the Bears demolished everybody in the playoffs, us included.

Tony Franklin gave us a quick 3-0 lead with a 36-yard field goal just 1:19 into the first quarter, but that was it for us. I don't know if we made the Bears angry by taking a lead on them or what, but they just took us apart after that first field goal.

McMahon ran for two touchdowns and passed for 256 yards, and Perry dominated up front, stopping our running game and harassing both of our quarterbacks all day long. Tony Eason couldn't get it going at all and was replaced with Steve Grogan in the second quarter. Steve had a rough day, too, taking four sacks and getting intercepted twice. But he gave us a small measure of respectability when he hit me with an 8-yard touchdown pass for New England's first—and, up until Super Bowl XXXI, only—Super Bowl touchdown. It was the only touchdown the Bears had allowed in the playoffs that year.

From the Mountaintop to the Valley

It took us three playoff games to establish ourselves as the team every fan loved to love. We were the underdogs, the overachievers. Our fans—and many fans around the nation—fell in love with us.

But it wasn't two days after our Super Bowl humiliation that the New England Patriots went from being loved as the "Rocky" of professional football to being reviled as a bunch of social outcasts.

This was during that embarrassing time when the Patriots organization was rocked by the post-Super Bowl drug scandal.

The Patriots had adopted a confidential drug counseling program prior to the 1985 season. Coach Berry had used mandatory drug testing on a few players and had dealt with some drug problems on the team. (That was his right, as long as he reasonably believed there was a problem.)

Following our loss to the Bears, Coach Berry called the team together and asked the players for help in cleaning up what he thought was a "drug problem" on the team. We voted to adopt a voluntary drug testing program, the first of its kind in the NFL. When the press found out about the vote, the immediate assumption was that the Patriots had a "drug problem." To make matters worse, General Manager Patrick Sullivan released the names of six players to the press who had admitted to Coach Berry that they had used drugs, violating the confidentiality that was one of the key conditions of the program. I was one of those players.

Coach Berry asked us to implement the drug testing program because he was concerned over drug use by his players, and the players agreed to it, only to have the press assume that we adopted the program because we had a serious drug problem on the team. We went from being AFC champions to being seen as a bunch of druggies, all in a span of two days.

The players were angered by what happened, and a couple of them even asked to be traded. In time, though, the furor died down and the Patriots were able to rub off the tarnish that had covered their image.

We went on to have another 11-5 season in 1986, this one good for the American Football Conference Eastern Division championship. Almost as soon as the drug scandal came up, it was forgotten. The Patriots had, to an extent, cleaned up their mess.

For me, though, my personal mess was just beginning.

CHAPTER SIX

LIVING WITH THE MESS
MY LIFE'S DOWNWARD SPIRAL

L et's go over to the other side of the lake," Jesus said to His disciples one day.

The Bible doesn't tell us if Jesus told them *why* He wanted to go to the other side of the lake, only that they all got in the boat and headed out to Gerasenes, across the lake from Galilee.

It was a pretty lengthy trip, and Jesus decided to lay down and take a nap as they sailed. The Bible says that as He lay there sleeping, a squall—a sudden, violent windstorm—came upon the lake. It must have been some storm, because the Word says that the wind and the waves started to swamp the boat, and the disciples were in danger of going down with their boat and drowning. Finally, they woke Jesus and said, "Master, Master, we're going to drown!"

While the disciples were in a state of panic, sure this was their last day on earth, Jesus was calm. He just stood up and surveyed the situation. Then, with all the authority and certainty befitting who He was as the Son of God, He simply told the wind and the raging water, "Be still!" In an instant, the wind stopped and the waves subsided. All was calm.

The Bible says that Jesus then turned to the disciples and simply asked them, "Where is your faith?" The disciples, now safe but still frightened and amazed at what they had just seen, talked among themselves, asking, "Who is this? He commands even the winds and the water, and they obey him."

The disciples spent all that time with Jesus but still didn't understand who He was or what He could do. Jesus could have calmed that storm at any moment, but it wasn't until their lives were in peril, until their deaths seemed like a certainty that they called out to Him to do something.

I think I understand how the disciples felt as they saw their lives flashing before their eyes as the water and wind threatened to take them to their deaths. You see, I went through a storm in my own life, a storm I thought would drag me down for good. There were times when I not only *thought* I would die, but *hoped* I would.

The difference between me and the disciples, though, is that I didn't have the sense to wake Jesus and ask Him to calm the storm. I didn't even know to call on Him to help me make sense of everything and quiet the wind and the waves that threatened to take me down for good.

I call this time in my life "the Mess."

This is what became of my life and my reputation during those tough times when I was living in Boston and playing for the New England Patriots. It was a time when there were stories about me concerning wife abuse, gambling, drinking, drug use, and weapons charges. Some of the things that were being said and written about me weren't true, but there were more than enough things being said and written that were. The truth was that my life was in shambles.

I wasn't living right. I wasn't honoring God, and I still hadn't acknowledged His calling on my life. I wasn't the kind of husband and father I needed to be. The immediate consequences were that I was branded a troublemaker, a punk, and a criminal. Some people in the local and national media even suggested that the Patriots should do their own image a favor and send me packing. Even our general manager publicly questioned my commitment to the team.

I was as confused as a man can be. I made bad decisions, hung out at the wrong places with the wrong people, and did the wrong things to my body. The devil was absolutely having his way with my mind, my career, and my marriage.

It was a time when I didn't have a clue as to how to turn things around.

A Lack of Foundation

The fact that I wasn't living for the Lord—that I didn't *know* the Lord—during my early years in the National Football League made me more vulnerable to yielding to the kinds of temptations every young NFL player faces. Without Him as my foundation, I had no idea how to deal with the things that were set before me. To make matters worse, I was still pretty naive.

When I first entered the league I had no idea what the NFL was all about. I didn't realize how important it was to people, how big NFL players become in their eyes. Up until my senior year in college, I hadn't thought all that much about playing in the NFL, and it wasn't something I planned for or prepared for. So when I got there, I was still just naive Irving Fryar, only now with a little money in my pocket.

There wasn't anybody, either, that I could turn to and ask such basic questions as, "Where do I go now?" "What do I do?" "How do I conduct myself?" "How do I invest my money?" Nobody came to me and told me what I should and shouldn't be doing or where I should and shouldn't be going, and nobody told me which people to avoid. None of my family or friends understood what I was facing, and nobody really took me under their wing to give me some guidance.

So I did what any naive rookie with no real guidance would do—I messed up. Big time.

We're all responsible for our own actions, and I know I'm no exception. I'm not trying to make excuses for the mistakes I made my first few years in the NFL. I simply didn't know how to handle the situations I found myself in, and I made a lot of mistakes because of that.

With each mistake I made, with each thing that happened to me, I fell deeper and deeper into my mess.

Problems at Home and in the Press

When you're not saved, or when you're not walking with the Lord as you should, you are wide open to Satan's attacks. If you're married, the first thing he will attack is your home. He's been doing that since the beginning of time, since Adam and Eve in the garden.

One of the first things that Satan attacked in my life in order to drag me into "the Mess" was my marriage. The first year of our marriage was far from wedded bliss. I truly loved Jacqui, but I had no idea what it took to make a marriage successful. Neither did she. We didn't understand what it took to live in harmony with one another.

Although Jacqui and I were having a lot of problems in our marriage, there was an attack on our marriage from outside that made things worse. It occurred just before the 1985 AFC championship game in Miami, a game I missed because of a badly cut finger.

Jacqui and I had been arguing when I cut my finger in an accident at home. I slammed a kitchen drawer, causing a knife caught in the back of the drawer to move forward in such a way that it badly sliced the little finger on my right hand. It was a bad cut, deep enough that one of the tendons was severed. It was bleeding like crazy, so I had to go immediately to get some medical attention.

Jacqui and I got in the car, and I did the best I could to drive with my cut and bleeding finger. Jacqui was pregnant with our first child, and she was getting upset over the situation, and we started arguing. Soon, my anger got the best of me, and I stopped the car, told her to get out, called a friend of Jacqui's to pick her up, and went on to the hospital myself.

Jacqui arrived at the hospital shortly after I got there, and she was upset. She'd been to the hospital probably three or four times before to make sure the baby was OK. Since it was her first child, she worried a lot about the pregnancy, so every time she felt something move, she'd go and get checked to make sure everything was OK. She was upset again by this time, so she went to get herself checked.

I got some attention for my finger, and Jacqui and I both went home. But that wasn't the end of it for either of us.

I ended up missing the AFC championship game with the injured finger, and I played but didn't start in Super Bowl XX. It was embarrassing to me to have to miss a playoff game because of a stupid accident, but the incident wasn't to be forgotten after the Super Bowl. I don't know exactly where the story came from, but on January 12, the day of the AFC championship game, the *Boston Globe* printed an article titled, "Fryar stabbing: the real story." The article reported that Jacqui had cut my hand during a fight we'd gotten into outside a restaurant in Boston. According to the article, the stabbing took place after an argument between Jacqui and me escalated in the restaurant and turned physical in the parking lot. I supposedly knocked Jacqui down, and she allegedly retaliated by reaching into her purse, pulling out a knife, and slashing at me. When I put my hand up to defend myself, the article said, my right hand was slashed.

Jacqui and I had our marital problems and we put one another through some really tough times during the early years of our marriage. But Jacqui *did not* pull a knife on me and cut me. That just didn't happen.

Seeing her name in the press in connection with a domestic stabbing hurt Jacqui deeply and it hurt me that she had to go through something like that. There were some brutal things written about her, too, things that still hurt her to think about.

Things were to get a lot worse for us before they got any better. It was just weeks after I cut my hand that my name was in the papers in connection with another scandal.

Accused of Gambling

The drug scandal surrounding the New England Patriots following our loss in Super Bowl XX wasn't the only scandal I was involved in following the 1985 season. It was around that time that I was also accused of gambling on the Super Bowl.

I'd been named to the AFC Pro Bowl team as a kick returner that season, and I went to Hawaii to play in the game. One night, Raymond Berry called me and said, "Irving, you've been accused of gambling, so expect the press to come to you asking questions." Raymond went on to explain what he'd been told so that I would be prepared for what was about to take place.

Instead of relaxing and enjoying a couple of days in Honolulu, I had to deal with questions from reporters. Again, my reputation took another hit in the press.

To this day, I still don't know how the gambling rumors got started. (Maybe it's a good thing that I don't.) It might have been because of the other things that were going on in my life at the time or part of my reputation as the NFL's Bad Boy. I do know that I never gambled on football. To me, this is another example of limits I had in my life. I knew better than to gamble on football. As a player in the NFL, you just don't do that. Besides, even at that point in my career, I had a sense of pride in the kind of work I was doing, and I wanted to—as best I could at the time—uphold the game.

I made a lot of mistakes during the course of my career, but the one thing I regret is that my name was never really cleared of the gambling charges. The league did a three-year investigation and found nothing to substantiate the rumors about me. But I never heard anyone say that I had been cleared of any wrongdoing. In fact, I never heard anything else said on the matter.

The gambling accusations were a fitting end to what had suddenly become a tough 1985 season for me. All I could hope for was a fresh start and a better year in 1986.

But it didn't happen.

Deeper into the Mess

When you look at the New England Patriots' record in 1986 and how I played personally, it would be easy to believe that I was at peace with everything that was going on.

On the field, we had just come off our Super Bowl season, and we were in the process of winning the franchise's first AFC divisional title since 1978 with an 11-5 record. I had a series of nagging injuries during training camp, and struggled in our games early that year, failing to catch a pass or return a punt our first two games. After I got healthy, I went through a time early in the season when it seemed like I was dropping more passes than I caught. But I started working extra hard in practice, catching at least 200 balls a day. Soon my confidence came back, and I started playing pretty well. I even went through a streak of six games where I dropped only one pass.

But beneath all that, there was a lot of turmoil in my life. What had been a miserable end to the 1985 season turned into an even more miserable 1986 campaign.

With the cut finger incident, the drug scandal, and the gambling accusations fresh in people's memories, I was established in people's minds as trouble walking, as an example of what was wrong with professional sports. I had a reputation, and not much was going to happen in 1986 to change it. In fact, if anything, it only got worse.

I was charged with assault in June of that year after an incident during a party Jacqui and I were attending. I had gotten angry at a friend of Jacqui's for something he said, and there was an altercation. The charges were later dropped.

Then came one of the all-time low points of my time in "the Mess."

We were playing the Buffalo Bills in a November game in Foxboro when I injured my shoulder on a play. Harold Jackson, our receivers coach, told me I shouldn't play the rest of the day, but I told him I felt good enough to play. So I went back in the game, only to aggravate the injury. I still wanted to stay in the game, but at halftime the trainers told me I was done for the day. I was angered because, at the time, I felt I was being held out of the game because I had some incentives in my contract. I insisted I could go back out and play, but the trainer said, "No, just get dressed and stay in."

As I was getting dressed, Jacqui came in the locker room, and we started arguing. I was already angry because I felt like I was being held out of the game, and getting into an argument with my wife was the last straw. I'd heard enough from everybody that day, and I was leaving. I was supposed to get dressed then go to the sidelines with my teammates for the second half of the game, but I stormed out of the locker room, got in my car, and sped away from the stadium.

As I was driving, Jacqui called me on the car phone and begged me to come back to the stadium. But I would not have it. As far as I was concerned, I was done with the Patriots. In my mind, they were trying to pull one over one me, and I wasn't going to put up with it. Jacqui's begging me to come back to the stadium soon turned into a shouting match between the two of us.

As I sped on my way to who-knows-where that afternoon, I missed a turn not far from the stadium and plowed my Mercedes Benz 500SL into a tree. I hit the tree dead-on at 60 miles per hour. The impact was so hard that I broke the steering wheel with my chest and cracked the windshield with my head. The car was totaled, with the front end of it wrapped around the tree and the back end stacked up over the rear tires.

The wreck was bad enough that I could very easily have been killed. But in another example of God looking out for me even though I wasn't honoring Him, the area around the car's front seat was still intact. The car was almost demolished, but the doors still opened and closed perfectly. I opened the door and fell out of the car and passed out. The next thing I remember was waking up in the hospital with a bad concussion and no other injuries. Although I thought I could play in our game against the New Orleans Saints the following week, I was held out.

This story—or references to it—have been printed in every newspaper in the Boston area and every sports magazine in the nation. Everybody in New England remembers the time when Irving Fryar left a game during the third quarter and almost killed himself running into a tree with his car. But there's a part to the story that was never told, and I think it's time I told it.

I hit the tree on purpose.

I was angry at my team, angry at my wife, and angry with life. I'd had it with everything and everybody, and I wanted to end it all right then and there. I was riding an emotional roller coaster, and my life was out of control. The way I saw it, there was only one answer. I was either going to die that day or get so badly injured that I wouldn't have to worry about football or anything else.

But God protected me that day.

That wasn't the only time I'd tried to take my own life. One off-season when Jacqui and I were living in Texas, I had come to a point when I couldn't take it any more. I was done with everything. I didn't care who it hurt or who I left behind. I was going to end it. I took a handful of prescription pills, got in the car, and drove off where I knew nobody would find me. I was just going to quietly go to sleep and not wake up.

But somehow Jacqui found me. She had no idea where I was going, but she went out looking for me and found me passed out in the car. She drove up in the parking lot where I was parked, and there I was.

It was only through the grace of God that I wasn't able to do what I'd set out to do. I was in rebellion, out of control, and ready to end it all. But God wasn't finished with me. He wasn't about to let me go. He had a calling on my life, and He wasn't going to give up on me until I acknowledged that calling and started walking in obedience to Him.

More Trouble

The New England Patriots struggled to achieve mediocrity during the two seasons following 1986, finishing 8-7 in a strike-shortened season in '87 and 9-7 in '88.

During those seasons I found myself getting in more trouble with the law, with my wife, and with the local news media.

There was one incident in 1987 when a little scandal broke out after I was robbed outside a downtown Boston jewelry store. I was still using drugs and getting involved in the same old junk that had been threatening to ruin my life since I came into the NFL. One day, I was walking out of the jewelry store with a bag containing some items I had purchased when a guy came up behind me, pushed me, and knocked the bag out of my hand. He grabbed the bag and started running, but I ran after him, caught and knocked him down, and got the bag back. The other robber then came after me in his car, and there was a shot fired. I walked away from the incident unhurt, but shaken up.

I wasn't going to file a report with the police, but Lou Assad, head of security with the Patriots, made me report it by bringing the police to practice the day after I had told him what happened. The police did an investigation of the scene, but couldn't find anything. The matter was dropped, and the police said they were suspicious about my report to them.

My cynicism and my anger—already dominating factors in my life— grew like a cancer.

In 1988 I was arrested in New Jersey on gun possession charges. I had a Massachusetts license for the guns but no New Jersey license. Actually, all I was doing was moving some of my things during the off-season, and I had my whole wardrobe in the car. When I was pulled over by a New Jersey state trooper for speeding, he found my 12-gauge shotgun, my .38-caliber handgun, and some ammunition.

I was charged with two counts each of illegal possession of weapons and possession of prohibited weapons and devices. I was released after posting bail. The charges were later thrown out, because I was in the process of moving. Although I was cleared of wrongdoing, it put yet another black spot on my reputation.

My Battle with Drugs

Adding to all my problems during those years I call "the Mess" was my use of cocaine. I started using cocaine after I finished playing football at Nebraska and prior to heading into my rookie year with the Patriots.

I was never physically addicted to cocaine. It wasn't something I did every day, and I didn't have to have it. There are people who get physically addicted, but it wasn't like that for me. It was just something I wanted, something that became a crutch for me. When a problem came up in my life that I didn't want to face, I used cocaine. When Jacqui and I had one of our arguments, I would disappear for a couple days and go on a cocaine binge.

Except for my second year in the NFL, I did a pretty good job of hiding my drug use, mostly because I didn't use that much during the football season. I would go the whole season without doing anything, but when the off-season came and a problem would come up, I would disappear for days on end.

Misery Loves Company

With all the garbage that was going on in my life, things became tougher and tougher for Jacqui and me. If I even so much as got pulled over for a traffic violation it was national news. One night, I got pulled over for doing 45 in a 35 mph zone, and the next day I was called by a newspaper in California. When Jacqui and I were out together at night, we overheard people say things about me, about her, and about the kind of people they thought we were.

I have made plenty of mistakes in my personal, professional, and public life. But the things that were being said and written about me hurt me and angered me. I got in trouble mostly because of my own stupidity and lack of direction in my life. But I still hated knowing that people thought of me as a bad person, as a trouble-ridden football player who was doing nothing but hurting the reputation of the New England Patriots. It also hurt me to know that Jacqui was suffering because of what had been going on in my life.

The stress of all that was going on—plus the fact that we both still had plenty to learn about married life—took its toll our marriage. We each had times where we'd had enough and wanted to get a divorce. But God held us together. Even though we weren't living for Him, God saw to it that at least one of us had enough calmness and sense to say the right thing at the right time to keep the marriage together.

Although we weren't happily married at this time, neither of us would never let the other one leave. When I wanted to go, she somehow said what she needed to keep me home. And when she wanted to leave, I was able to persuade her to stay.

We may have been miserable, but we were miserable together.

I loved my wife and my children. I couldn't stand the thought of them suffering because of my mistakes. So I decided the best thing to do was run away from my problems, to leave New England and start over somewhere else.

Trade Me!

It seemed like every season I was trying to get out of New England. I walked up to Coach Berry or Pat Sullivan many times and said, "I want to be traded." But they wouldn't trade me.

When my first contract expired, I didn't want to re-sign with the Patriots, but they wouldn't let me go. This was before the age of unrestricted free agency, where a player can sign with anybody who can afford him after his contract runs out. Back then, you had to re-sign with your team, or you sat out a year. I ended up signing with New England again.

As hard as I tried to get out of New England, Coach Raymond Berry wouldn't let me go. He wouldn't trade me, and he wouldn't let me sign with another team. Yet he continued playing me, and he never fined me.

You might think that a coach like Raymond Berry would want to be rid of someone who was living the way I was. Looking back, I think there was more going on in this situation than I could have understood at the time. I really believe that God was speaking to Coach Berry to keep me around. God had work to do in my life, and He wanted to do it in New England. Coach Berry, being a praying Christian man, kept giving me chances where other coaches would have given me my walking papers.

I hated being in New England. I was in a place where people saw me as a troublemaker and a petty criminal. It was a tough place to be, emotionally and physically. I was tired of all the bad things that were being said and written about me. I wanted some kind of peace in my life. I wanted to be in a place where I wouldn't be the center of attention for the local media and where I wouldn't be referred to as "troubled" Irving Fryar.

But I couldn't get out of New England. I couldn't run away from my problems. So I did the next best thing. I hid.

Hiding Out

I decided during the 1988 season that I wasn't going to let anybody near me. I didn't talk to people or go out or do much of anything during that time. I just went to practice, went home, then played football on Sunday afternoons. I isolated myself—as much as an NFL player can, anyway—and stayed away from people. I didn't go out partying. I didn't talk to the media. I just kept a low profile, hoping no one would notice I was there.

As tough as it was to be getting into trouble and having to listen to all the bad things that were being said about me, isolating myself like that wasn't a whole lot easier. I wanted to make some changes in my life, at least try to be a better person. But I didn't know where to turn or who to talk to in order to make some real life changes.

I didn't trust anybody, and nobody trusted me. I was basically on my own. So I did what I could to live what I'd always thought was a good life.

In a sense, my strategy worked. I didn't get into even minor trouble. No arrests, no scandals, no accusations. I may have been lonely, empty, and miserable, but I also wasn't seeing my name in the newspapers in connection with some kind of trouble.

I had, by the world's standards, "cleaned up" my life. I stopped using drugs and drinking, and started spending more time at home with my wife and kids. It looked like I had turned my life around.

But God wanted more. He wasn't satisfied with me just giving up the partying, the drugs, and the drink. He didn't want me to just live a good life. He wanted me. All of me. I had been trying to get my act together, but without the help of the Lord. I'd tried to give Him parts of myself, but God wanted it all. He wanted my mind, my body, my marriage, my career. If there was anything I had, God wanted it.

The same God who had called me so many years before and who had followed me from my boyhood home in Mount Holly, New Jersey, to college in Lincoln, Nebraska, was about to put me in a position where I had but one choice: surrender.

CHAPTER SEVEN

CLEANING UP THE MESS
HOW I MET THE LORD JESUS

Hey, man, let's go talk after practice."

I was a little surprised to hear those words coming from this rookie wide receiver from Penn State. It isn't often that a first-year player would have the courage to invite a veteran out just to talk about life.

That rookie was Michael Timpson, who to this day is my best friend (and my teammate with the Philadelphia Eagles) in the NFL. It was during the 1989 season that Michael approached me and asked me if I wanted to talk. It was my sixth season in the league and his first.

My talk with Michael was the start of some big changes in my life. As strange as it may sound, this rookie actually planted a seed in my life, a seed—like the seeds that had been planted by Tom Osborne and Raymond Berry—that would one day grow. Michael started talking to me about my life, what he saw in me, and what I should be doing differently. To this day, I can see no earthly reason why I listened to him. I mean, who was he to tell me how to live? He was a rookie, and I was an established veteran. If anyone should have been telling the other how to live, it should have been me telling him. But I listened to him. For some reason, I had to.

"Man, I know you're a good person," Michael said. "Sometimes you try to put up a facade and try to be tough. But I see some good things in you."

Michael went on to tell me what he thought about the things he'd heard about me and what I should do to clean up my life and my reputation. He didn't give me any solid spiritual advice—he hadn't totally committed his life to Christ at that point—but he spoke common sense, something I lacked then.

This talk I had with Michael Timpson was during a time when I just got fed up with the trouble I was getting myself into and the things that were being said and written about me. I may have done a lot of foolish things, but I had enough sense to know that I had to make some changes. For the better part of two years, that's exactly what I did.

I had been living a "cleaned up" life, avoiding the clubs, the drugs, and the controversy that seemed to be so much a part of my life during my first five years in the NFL. Things had been quiet for me at home and in public for almost two years. No arrests, no scandals, and no blowups with my wife and kids.

Although things were going better for Jacqui and I, there was still something missing in our lives, something that God wanted us to have.

We weren't saved yet, but we were definitely thinking about what role we wanted God to play in our lives. We were thinking about God, but we hadn't made any commitment to Him or what He wanted for us. In short, He didn't have our attention as much as He wanted.

God got our attention on April 22, 1990, the day our first daughter, Adrianne, was born.

A Rough Start

Adrianne was our third child. Our first son, Londen, was a month away from his fourth birthday, and our second son, Irving, Jr., was four months short of his third birthday when Adrianne was born. Our two boys were born in Stoneham, Massachusetts, and both were as healthy as any parent could hope for. Adrianne, born in Rhode Island, was a very sick little girl for her first two years of life.

Having already had two healthy kids, it never crossed our minds that our third child would be any different. We just assumed everything was going to be fine with our third baby.

It was a wrong assumption.

I was in the delivery room with Jacqui for Adrianne's birth. The doctors had induced labor and everything seemed to be going fine. Before I knew what was going on, that changed. The doctors had to do an emergency

Caesarean section because the umbilical cord had gotten wrapped around the baby's neck.

All of a sudden, there were several doctors in the room working on Adrianne. I had no idea what was going on. All I could do was look around and ask, "Who are you?!" "What are you doing?!" I knew there was something very wrong.

The next thing I know, they're rushing Adrianne and Jacqui out of the delivery room and into the emergency room. I still didn't know what was wrong, only that they wouldn't let me go in the emergency room with my wife and daughter.

It's hard for people who haven't gone through something like this with their child to understand the feelings of fear and panic that come over you in a situation like this. In a short space of time, I went from a happily expectant father to a man who didn't even know if his daughter was alive, let alone healthy. To make matters worst, I was alone.

I stayed outside the emergency room, hoping for the best but fearing the worst. After what seemed like an eternity, one of the emergency room staff came out.

"Is the baby OK?" I asked, wanting desperately to know but deathly afraid of the answer I might get.

"Mr. Fryar," the doctor said, "we don't think it's anything serious. Your daughter has a heart murmur, but it's nothing to worry about. A lot of people have heart murmurs. We're going to check her out some more, but we think she's going to be fine."

They brought out Jacqui and let me see her for a few minutes before they wheeled her to the recovery room. She was physically and emotionally spent from what she had just gone through, but she was going to be OK.

At this point, I was feeling a mixture of relief and shock over what had just happened. I'd never been through anything like this before, and I was a bundle of emotion. I sat in the hospital by myself, wanting desperately to have somebody to talk to. Just then Jacqui's father walked in, and I rushed over to him and hugged him and cried. It felt good to see somebody who might have a clue what I was going through—another father.

Adrianne's Next Step

The doctor let us take Adrianne home, but told us that we needed to make an appointment and take her to Boston Children's Hospital to have some additional testing done—just to make sure everything was fine. Within a week after Adrianne came home with us, we took her to the hospital to have the tests done.

The doctor did a battery of tests to check out how Adrianne's heart was working. When the tests were finished, the doctor came out to talk to us. We knew from the moment we saw him that it wasn't good news.

"We have to admit your daughter *right now,*" he said, the urgency of the situation in his voice.

"What's the problem?" I asked, surprised by what the doctor was telling me, and mostly unprepared for any more bad news.

The doctor explained to us that Adrianne had two holes in her heart, a valve missing, and two pulmonary arteries that weren't connected. One of the pulmonary arteries was extremely oversized, and the other had no blood flow at all. The doctor explained that Adrianne needed an operation to connect the pulmonary arteries, close the holes, and replace the missing valve. In other words, Adrianne Fryar, my first daughter, would need major open-heart surgery before she was even two weeks old. The surgery would have been done the next day, except there was a delay before she could have her heart surgery.

Jacqui and I waited in the hospital that day as the doctors continued their tests on Adrianne, and then decided to go home and get a shower and a change of clothes. Upon our return to the hospital—three or four hours later—Jacqui was looking at Adrianne and thinking about what her little daughter would be going through the next day when she noticed there was blood in Adrianne's diaper.

Jacqui was the first one to see the blood, and we still thank God that she did, because it was the symptom of another problem that might have killed Adrianne if the operation had gone forward that next day.

After my wife saw the blood, the doctors did some more tests to find out what was wrong. It turns out that the blood was from a serious problem with

Adrianne's intestines that came about because of her heart. Her heart problems caused a deficiency in the blood flow—and, consequently, an oxygen
deficiency—to her bowels, which caused a piece of her bowel to die. So,
before Adrianne could get her heart repaired, she had to endure a surgery to
remove a four-inch piece of her intestine.

She also had to endure a rough two-week recovery from the surgery.
Adrianne, not even old enough to know where she was or who was around
her, had to wear a colostomy bag for the entire two weeks.

It was rough on that little girl to have to endure what was happening to
her little body at such a young age. But it was also a time when I came to
appreciate the inner strength of my wife. During the two weeks following the
surgery on her bowel, Adrianne's colostomy bag had to be changed regularly.
She was home for those two weeks, so Jacqui took care of it. Jacqui took care
of it because, frankly, I couldn't.

Whenever Jacqui would change the colostomy bag, the old one would
stick to Adrianne's skin, causing her horrendous pain when Jacqui removed
it. When Jacqui changed the bag, Adrianne would struggle and scream in
pain. All I could do was hold her and whisper words of comfort to her. Jacqui
and I both hurt for our child, but somehow my beautiful wife found an inner
strength—a strength that I couldn't find—to do what had to be done. I have
always loved my wife, even in the roughest, toughest parts of our marriage.
But seeing how she handled the situation with our first daughter made me
realize how special and strong she is.

I thanked God, a God I really didn't know at the time, for giving me such
a woman as my wife. Despite the tough time I was going through with my
daughter, I truly felt like a blessed man.

After two weeks of recovery from her abdominal surgery, Adrianne went
back to Boston Children's Hospital for her heart surgery. Her first heart
surgery was successful, but it would be the first of a series of surgeries she
would need to correct the problem.

At that point, it looked like Adrianne was going to pull through. As for
Jacqui and me, this brought us closer than we'd ever been and taught us
something about the God we didn't yet know. We still hadn't committed our

lives to Christ at the time this all happened, but I still felt the need to do something I hadn't done in years, something that I'd learned about as a boy from my grandmother, and something I actually did from time to time in church.

It was during this difficult time with my daughter that I actually prayed. I knew I hadn't lived right, and I knew I didn't have a relationship with God. Yet, here I was sitting in a hospital by myself. And I did what seemed to come naturally. I called out to God to save my little girl.

To this day, I don't know if God directly answered my prayer to let my daughter live, or if He just allowed her to stay with Jacqui and me because of His graciousness and mercy, or if He was answering the prayers of someone else who knew Him and was living right before Him.

There is one thing I realized then, and it's something I've never forgotten: God didn't have to save my baby, but He did. He didn't have to help me and Jacqui to successfully endure what we were going through, but He did. If God had wanted to be completely fair, He would have taken my daughter home and never allowed me to enjoy having her to hold and play with and love and smile at. If it had been simply a matter of an eye for an eye and a tooth for a tooth, God would have called my daughter home before she ever had a chance to know her daddy and mommy, before we'd ever have a chance to hold her and tell her how much we love her. But He didn't do that. Why did God allow my little girl to live beyond those first few months of life? Because of His mercy and grace. Because He had a plan for Adrianne, Jacqui, and me. It was a plan that revolved around me getting to know Him as my Lord and Savior.

I learned that God demonstrates His grace and mercy for us, not because of what we are or who we are but because of who He Himself is. It is in His nature to love us, to reach out to us—even when we've gone astray. There's no other reason for it. I deserved to be cut off because of the way I was living. We all do. But instead of turning His back on me because I'd turned my back on Him and denied my calling, He extended His mercy to me through my daughter.

And it wasn't long after my daughter's first few months of life that God reached down, pulled me out of another one of my self-inflicted messes, and made me one of His own children.

Into the Belly of the Fish

Almost two years had gone by since I'd had even a hint of the trouble that had dominated my life during those years I call "the Mess" when I decided one night in October of 1990 to go out for a nice, relaxing evening with Hart Lee Dykes, one of my New England Patriot teammates.

This night out was completely innocent. The club we visited, Club Shalimar in Providence, Rhode Island, featured a disc jockey who worked at a radio station I was trying to buy. *No problem*, I thought. *I'll just go out and have a few drinks, check out this deejay, and hang out with my friend.*

Hart Lee and I were the only black people in the club, but that didn't matter to us. We were having a good time, having a few drinks, and listening to the music.

I don't know exactly how it started, but Hart Lee got into an argument with some people at the bar about the Patriots. We were in the midst of an awful 1-15 season, and someone was giving Hart Lee some grief about it. Professional athletes are supposed to know how to handle situations like this, but Hart Lee apparently didn't. Pretty soon, the argument turned ugly. One thing led to another, things started to get out of hand, and the next thing I know Hart Lee and I were outside the club with about five other guys and a fight broke out.

These guys were really whipping on Hart Lee, and somebody hit him over the head with a crutch. It seemed like it was just me and him out there against everybody else in the club, and I was genuinely worried that these guys were going to kill him. I didn't know what to do, so I went to my car and got my pistol and put it in my boot.

When I got back to the scene of the fight, people started spreading out and backing away from me because they knew I was armed. I bent down to get the gun—I had no intention of shooting anybody; I just wanted to scare people away from Hart Lee before they killed him—and when I did, somebody hit me over the head with a baseball bat. The blow made a nasty gash on my head, and the blood started flowing. Fortunately, I stayed conscious. If I'd been knocked unconscious, Hart Lee and I could have been hurt much worse. (The doctors told us later that Hart Lee was about one more blow to the head away from losing his sight in one eye.)

Somehow, I was able to get Hart Lee up from the pavement and drag him to the car. We got there, both of us bleeding badly, just about the time the Providence police showed up. An ambulance arrived in short order to take Hart Lee to the hospital. Me, I had another destination that night.

I wanted to cooperate with the police, so I walked up to one of them and said, "Officer, I have a gun in my boot. I have a license for it, but I thought I'd better tell you." Since I had a license for my gun and had been trained to handle it correctly, I didn't think there would be a problem as long as I told the police I had it. I thought I was doing the right thing, and I probably was. But the results weren't what I'd expected.

I was arrested and charged with carrying a weapon without a Rhode Island permit. My license was for Massachusetts, so I would be spending what proved to be a very pivotal night of my life alone in a Providence jail cell.

Still bleeding from my little meeting with that Louisville Slugger outside Club Shalimar, I was driven to the courthouse in Providence and led to the jail cell. The arresting officers had taken my shirt because it was soaked with blood—mine and Hart Lee's. I tried to call my attorney, but for some reason I couldn't reach him. The police wouldn't let me make another call, but put me back in my cell and said, "We're going to call your attorney for you. What's the number?" I gave them the number, and a short time later an officer told me, "We reached your attorney, and he's on his way here."

But my attorney never showed up. Nobody showed up. I was on my own that night, still bleeding from a cut that wouldn't be stitched shut until the next morning. By this time, the effects of the drinks I'd had were wearing off, and my head started to throb horribly. But the pain didn't stop me from doing some heavy-duty thinking. And it certainly didn't stop God from dealing with me, either.

Going Down and Hitting Bottom

That night, I officially hit rock bottom. Like Jonah when he ran from God's calling, I'd been going steadily down. Despite my disobedience and despite the fact that I had turned my back on God, He had blessed me in my football career and with a beautiful wife and children. I had everything a man could want, yet my life was an absolute mess.

Over the past two years, I'd cleaned up the way I was living somewhat, and I hadn't gotten in any trouble for quite a while. The only time my name had appeared in the paper during that time was in relation to football. But now I was right back where a lot of people thought I belonged anyway: in jail. All that "clean living" that I'd done the previous two years was down the drain, and with it what shred of a reputation I had built for myself the previous two years.

I thought about what had just happened, and I dreaded what my wife would say, what the Patriots' coach, Rod Rust, would say, and what the papers would say. I thought about how quiet my life had been for almost two years, and how this one night would bring back to everyone's memory all the garbage that had taken place in my life before. *My wife will probably want to leave me, the Patriots will want to cut me, and the people in New England will again brand me a troublemaker and a criminal,* I thought. It just didn't seem fair.

Here I was in jail, in the belly of a great fish that God had prepared especially for me, simply because I refused to turn my life over to Him. At that point, I realized that I was tired of running, tired of fighting, tired of the mess. I was through with it. Something had to change. I'd tried everything else, and my life was miserable. So I called out to God. Right there in that little jail cell, sitting on a cold metal bench, I called out to the same God who, according to Alice Oakman, my grandmother, had called me to preach.

I don't remember specifically what I prayed, but I knew to Whom I was praying. It was Jesus Christ. I remember very vividly just crying out and praying something like this: "Lord, I'm tired of all this junk in my life. I can't go on like this. There have been times in my life when I woke up in the morning and didn't want to be here, but for some reason unknown to me, You continued to get me up each day and help me get through it all. But something has to change and it has to change now. I don't have any answers any more. I can't go on any more. Do what You have to to change me."

I remember how much peace there was inside me after I prayed. I knew I would still have to face the music the next day, but I wasn't worried about it any more. Now God was in control. Everything was going to be OK.

The next morning the papers, the television and radio stations, and everybody else were waiting outside the jail house when I came out. When I went into the courtroom, they were all waiting. But when I went to court that day, I wasn't worried at all. I knew God was now in control and that He was going to take care of everything.

The charges against me were later dropped because I had a Massachusetts license to carry my gun, and it covered Rhode Island. That part of this episode was behind me, but God still wasn't finished with my transformation. I had one more big step to take.

How I Found Jesus Christ

The peace that God had given me the night of my arrest mostly stayed with me through the next couple of months. I still struggled at times with the enemy trying to steal my peace (which he did at different times), because I didn't know how Satan works and that his main objective is to steal the peace of God.

I hadn't fully committed my life to Christ that night in the jail cell. Basically, I let Him know that I was going to be looking for Him and trying to figure out what it took to have Him take complete control in my life. I guess you could say I was still searching for God. I had written Him an IOU, and I intended to honor it.

And the great thing about honestly and sincerely searching for God is that He'll always allow you to find Him.

Jacqui and I had been attending church but not with any great regularity. We repeatedly heard about another church, a church where people worshiped God, where people were getting saved, getting healed, getting delivered. Things were happening there! This church was located in the Roxbury section of Boston, and it had a young pastor by the name of William Dickerson. It was called Greater Love Tabernacle Ministries.

I was formally invited to the church one day when I went to a community center in the Roxbury area to speak to some youths. Before I spoke, I got in a conversation with a man who, it turns out, was a deacon at Greater Love Tabernacle Ministries. He told me they were having services in that very community center, and invited me to come the next Sunday morning. Without hesitation, I told him, "I'll be there."

I don't think this man believed that I would be there on Sunday, but I was. And I loved what I saw. I loved the freedom of their worship, and I loved how real God seemed to these people. So I came back.

The following Friday was Good Friday, and I went to the church's service. That's where God got hold of me in a way that I never thought possible. That's where He put His mark on me and claimed me as one of His own.

I went to church that Friday by myself (Jacqui and the kids were out of town). I don't remember exactly what Rev. Dickerson preached, but one message came through loud and clear, as if it were directed specifically at me: *You need Jesus!*

I'd gone to church many times in my life—in high school, in college, and during my years in pro football—and it had always been tough on me when they gave the altar call. I always knew that I should walk up there and give my life to Jesus, but something always held me back. I wasn't ready to humble myself and ask God to forgive me.

This time, though, nothing was going to keep me from that altar. I got up from my seat in the back of the church, made my way down the aisle, and, with tears in my eyes, told Rev. Dickerson that I wanted Jesus to save and cleanse me.

I don't know if the pastor put his hands on me when he prayed. All I remember is him praying, "Father, in the name of Jesus..." and I was on the floor. It was like somebody had hit me on the forehead and knocked me backwards so quickly that my feet flew out from under me.

In an instant, I was flat on my back and I realized that I was saying or praying something that I couldn't understand. I was speaking in tongues! Before that day, nobody could have told me that speaking in tongues was for real. I always figured it was just a bunch of gibberish coming out of the mouths of people whose emotions had gotten the better of them.

As I lay there, totally overcome by what God was doing to me, I thought, *What's happening to me? Why am I on the floor? This isn't me!* I'd never been one to put a lot of stock in this kind of thing. Before this I didn't really know about what it means to give my life to Christ. And I knew nothing of the Holy Spirit. All I knew was that Jesus was supposed to be the Son of God and that He came to earth to save us.

God didn't seem to care too much what I understood, what I had believed in, what I'd thought He could do, or how I'd thought He could do it. It was time for me to step back and let Him do what He wanted. And let me tell you, the Spirit of God was all over me.

I didn't know what was happening to me, only that there was an amazing sense of peace that flooded my whole being. It was like all the junk that had ever been a part of my life was being swept away and replaced by the love and peace of Jesus Christ.

I was on that community center floor for about thirty minutes before I got up—before I *could* get up. When I finally got to my feet, I knew something had changed inside me, and I knew that the change was for real and permanent. All the junk that had been inside me—the drugs, the alcohol, the lies, and the turmoil—didn't all just disappear at once. But now there was a game plan for me. And, most of all, there was the Holy Spirit dwelling inside me and giving the strength and motivation I needed to change.

Sticking with It

After that, I kept going back to church. I was there every time the doors opened. I even joined the choir. At first, Jacqui wasn't coming with me, but with me being in church so much it was only a matter of time before she joined me. One day, I was in church and she showed up. I was glad to see her, but a little surprised that she'd just show up like that.

"What are you doing here?" I asked her.

"Well, lately the only way I can see you is to come to church," she said.

So come to church is exactly what she did. She came the next Sunday and joined the church, and on May 19, 1991—our son Londen's fifth birthday—Jacqui committed her life to the Lord Jesus Christ. Since that time, we've both grown together in our love for Him and our love for one another.

And we've also grown together as we've pursued that calling God put on my life from the very start.

Endnote

I'm happy to report that our little girl, Adrianne, even though she got off to a rough start, is doing very well now.

She had two other surgeries after her initial heart surgery when she was an infant. The surgeon did some pretty extensive work, repairing the holes in her heart, repairing the arteries, and replacing the valve. But now she's healthy and active, just like our other kids. The only medicine she takes regularly is an aspirin a day.

It's so exciting to see her grow and do the things little girls like to do. Her mother was a jazz dancer before I married her, and now Adrianne has followed in Mom's footsteps and become my little dancer. My precious little daughter loves to dance so much that she often stands in front of the big-screen television set when it's not on, just so she can see herself in the glass.

CHAPTER EIGHT

OUT WITH THE OLD, IN WITH THE NEW

ACKNOWLEDGING MY CALLING

When I called out to God to save me, I surrendered my old way of living and thinking as I received a new life and a renewed mind. I surrendered a whole lot more than that when I first met Jesus Christ that Good Friday in Boston.

I surrendered myself.

My whole self.

In addition to acknowledging to God that I needed Him to save me and cleanse me, I had to concede one other thing: His calling on me to preach. It was that same calling that my grandma had told me about when I was a boy in Mount Holly and it was the same calling that had followed me all the years I was in rebellion. It was this same calling I had to acknowledge when I asked Jesus to be my Lord and Savior.

When I submitted to my calling I saw big changes in my life. Changes people could see and hear, and changes only I knew about. Changes in how I treated my wife and children, and changes in how I treated my body. Changes in the people I spent my time with and changes in the things I did.

One of the first changes I made was to give up an outward sign of my inward rebellion. After I prayed at the altar and told God that I was no longer going to run from my calling, I took out my earring and handed it to Rev. Dickerson.

There isn't anything necessarily wrong with wearing an earring, but there was something wrong with what it stood for in my life. To me, my earring stood for the world and for the things that I had been doing when I was in the world. It stood for my pride. When I started wearing an earring, I did it because I wanted to look good and because all my friends were wearing them. To me, wearing an earring was all about me trying to be like the people I was running around with and partying with.

When I gave in to God's calling on me to preach, it occurred to me that Jesus didn't do the things He did because He saw everybody else doing it. He did everything so he could glorify His Father and draw people to Himself. I wanted to glorify my heavenly Father, and I just couldn't see myself standing in the pulpit wearing an earring or preaching to others that their lives had to change while I still had a symbol of my old life dangling in my ear. So it had to go.

A lot of things had to go.

Inner Cleansing

The early days of my salvation were times of radical change and a time when the Spirit of God was dealing with me, giving me a sensitivity and compassion for people that I'd never had before. I was acutely sensitive to the Holy Spirit and would cry at the drop of a hat. When I saw a homeless person on a street corner, I would walk over and empty my pockets of every cent I was carrying, then say "God bless you" and walk away crying like a baby.

Mostly, they were times when God worked inside me to rid my life of the garbage that had dragged me down all those years.

One of the first things He started with was the drugs and alcohol. I started smoking marijuana early in my teenage years, and I first used cocaine right after I finished my college football career with Nebraska. During those years of the "the Mess" I was hitting it hard, too, spending a lot of time and money on drugs.

I had pretty much stopped using drugs during the year and a half leading up to my arrest that October night. But God didn't want to just help me quit, He wanted to cleanse me and deliver me.

Although God's Spirit was on me heavily, helping me to overcome the old life, it was still a struggle to leave the drug-abusing lifestyle.

When you give up something that is a big part of your life, there's always a struggle. For example, if you smoke cigarettes for years and then quit, you struggle with cigarettes because you know what it's like to smoke. After you quit, you may still have the desire to smoke, especially during certain times or in certain situations. If you do give in and have a cigarette, you would soon be back to the habit of smoking. That's the bondage of an addiction.

There was a time even after I was saved when I struggled with the desire to use cocaine. In fact, that was my toughest struggle because of what cocaine had done to my body and mind. Cocaine addiction was never really a physical thing for me, but a way to deal with my problems or something to do with my friends during certain times of the year. It was an emotional or mental addiction for me. For a few years after I was saved, it seemed like every year around a certain time I would get an itch and want to go out and play. I thought about it because I had done it before. But I knew better than to give in and use again. I knew that it was wrong, and I knew that if I did it, I'd be right back where I'd started.

I still realize that I can't go back to using cocaine. I know that if I were to do it today I'd be right back at it as bad as ever, because my mind and body remember it and can pick it back up in an instant.

The good news, though, is that I'm so busy now having a good time serving God that I don't have time to think about my desire for drugs or any of the other junk that I had in my life before I found Jesus.

To me, that's the key to victory over sin in my life. It isn't trying to win through willpower or any other human effort. The key is to replace the sin with something else. And God has given me plenty to replace the old things in my life. He has helped me to overcome my desire for my old ways by first giving me His Spirit, then by allowing me to know Him through His Word and through prayer.

There's an old saying that says, "Idle hands are the devil's workshop," and it applied to me before I knew Christ. In a spiritual sense, I did a lot of sitting around back then, and it caused me all kinds of problems. I ended up hanging out with the wrong people and doing the things that they were doing. But once I found God, I realized I didn't need the drugs or the alcohol to be happy or at peace. There was a better way.

God saved me, cleansed me, and called me to preach. He also showed me what it meant to be the kind of husband and father He wanted me to be. It didn't happen overnight, I'm still working on it, in fact, but God gave Jacqui and me a game plan for our marriage.

Changes in the Home

My wife couldn't have been happier when I first announced to her that I'd been saved and that I was going to preach, and that there would be big changes in me from that day forward. At the same time, though, she was a little wary. She'd been through enough with me to know about my mood swings and my erratic behavior. She wanted to see if this was for real.

As time went on, Jacqui could see the changes in me were real and lasting and that I wasn't just going through some kind of phase in my life. As she saw that, she came to trust in me as her husband and as the father of her children. When Jacqui surrendered her own life to Christ, we soon had a foundation on which to build the kind of home where she and I and our children could thrive.

God showed me quickly after I got saved that the most important thing in having a happy marriage and family life is reading and obeying the Bible, the Word of God. As I've come to know the Lord and come to understand what He wants from me, I've become the kind of father and husband He wants me to be. And I've gotten my directions from the Word of God.

The most important verse in the Bible that relates to my marriage is Galatians 6:7: "Be not deceived: God cannot be mocked. A man reaps what he sows."

I have a personal saying I tell young people when I preach, simply—you reap what you sow: *If you always do what you've always done, you'll always get what you've always gotten.*

How does that relate to my marriage? It's simple, really. To me, this means that if I sow love, I'll reap love. If I sow anger and division, anger and division is exactly what I'll get back. For example, if I stay out late night after night (like I used to), I know when I get home Jacqui is going to be upset with me, and there's going to be an interruption in the peace in our home. But if I make Jacqui and the kids my number one earthly priority—even ahead of my ministry—I know that I'm going to reap the rewards of being the kind of husband and daddy God wants me to be.

The Word also gives us husbands some instruction that is specifically aimed at our marriages. It says in Ephesians 5:25: "Husbands, love your wives, just as Christ loved the church and gave himself up for her..."

That verse tells us men that we are to love our wives as Jesus loved His church. And what did Jesus do for the church? *He sacrificed Himself!* It hasn't always been an easy process for me, but God has worked in my life and in Jacqui's to teach us how to live in harmony with one another as husband and wife. He's done that by teaching me the importance of the word *sacrifice*.

During the days of "the Mess" I loved my wife. Even though our relationship was full of conflict and misery and even though I was out doing the wrong things, I loved Jacqui deeply. But I was so wrapped up in myself and my own problems and my own misery that I couldn't begin to give my wife and my kids the kind of attention they needed. They didn't come before the other things in my life as they should have. I just didn't understand the idea of sacrificing myself for my family at that time.

It's not that hard to understand what the word *sacrifice* means in this context. It means one thing and one thing only: After God, your wife and your kids have got to come first. When we put that in perspective, we can have a great marriage and a great relationship with our kids.

As a man who is trying to be the most godly father he can be, I also look to the Word for wisdom in raising my four kids. One of my favorite verses in the Bible sums up how I see my responsibility as a father like this: "Train up a child in the way he should go, and when he is old he will not depart from it" Proverbs 22:6. It simply tells me to teach my kids right from wrong and to love God more than anything in their lives and to obey Him at all costs.

I always tell my kids not to be worried about anything but honoring their mother and father. I tell them, "Your job is just to do what God says to do, and that is to be obedient to your mother and me. I'm here to take care of you and teach you God's ways, but, ultimately, God is your Father. And if you're disobedient to me, then you're being disobedient to God."

That approach works for me for one reason: My kids see the love of their heavenly Father flowing to them through me. They see that because I have the love of Jesus Christ in my life.

At the time of this writing, Jacqui and I have been married for almost thirteen years, and let me tell you, our relationship has never been better. What's even more exciting is that it's going to continue to improve as the years go on, getting better because we're both growing in our love for God and learning to lean on Him more for the things we need to make our marriage better.

God has saved my marriage and made it great because I turned to Him and allowed Him to save me and clean out all the garbage in my life. As He did the same thing in my professional life, things changed at work, too.

A New Life in the NFL

My first full season in the National Football League as a saved man was 1991, when I was still playing for the New England Patriots. At first, I kept my salvation experience to myself. I didn't tell anybody what had happened to me that off-season. I wasn't ashamed of Jesus; I just wanted to get myself established, because I was just a little baby Christian then.

But the word soon got out: Irving Fryar had a "religious experience" and he wants to be a preacher! That was a big surprise to the guys who knew me during the tough times in my life. Some of them just plain didn't believe it. They thought I was just being the same old Irving, only with religion instead of drugs.

I don't remember which guys said it, but word got back to me that some of my teammates had their doubts that I'd stick with the commitment I made. They were saying, "Just give him another month, and he'll be back out there doing the same things he was doing before." To these guys, I was just going through another "phase," and that, too, would pass.

I can't say I blame them for thinking that. These were some of the same guys I had partied with, and all of them knew about my track record. They knew about my struggles with drugs, my marital problems, and my arrest record. They knew about my mood swings, my erratic behavior, and my disappearing acts.

But what they didn't know about was the experience I'd had that year. They didn't understand what had happened to me when I walked forward in that Boston church or that the Spirit of God had fallen so heavily on me that I was knocked off my feet. They didn't understand that the same Holy Spirit who came upon me that day still dwelt within me, giving me the power to change. They didn't understand the power of Jesus Christ to heal, to cleanse, and to save. And they didn't understand that it wasn't just a phase, but that I was a new man, a new Irving Fryar.

But it wasn't long before they realized that what had happened in my life was more than a phase. Much more.

My skeptical teammates saw that what had happened in my life was real through one thing: the life I was now living. Soon they realized that I was serious, that I was going to be serving Jesus Christ in my life.

The following season—1992—the same guys who were saying that I had just been going through a phase with this "religious conversion" started getting apologetic around me whenever they'd curse, swear, or say something they considered dirty or blasphemous. Whenever they'd say something like that around me, they'd stop and say, "I'm sorry, Irving. Please excuse me." What's really amazing about that is that before God saved me, I myself had a mouth like a sewer! I wasn't as bad as some of the guys, but I was bad enough. I'd spouted more than my share of filth around these same guys. Now they were apologizing for talking around me the same way!

It took a whole year for them to realize that I was serious about what I was doing. It had nothing to do with anything I said to them, either. I hadn't really talked to anybody on the team about Jesus at that point. I hadn't set anybody down and said, "This is what happened to me." But these football players, these guys who could curse and swear like longshoremen, stopped using foul language around me.

They saw something different in me because I certainly hadn't said much. They saw the difference in how I carried myself and how I walked with an attitude of peace and love. They saw Jesus in me. It amazed me that just seeing a difference in me made such an impression on my teammates.

I'm glad that God helped me to prove my teammates wrong about their skepticism. I never felt that I had to prove these guys wrong, because I believed what I believed and I was doing what I was doing. This was the life that God had called me to, and I was going to live it the best I could with His help. But I also can't help but think that seeing where I'd come from and how far I'd come somehow influenced some of my teammates. They may not have turned their lives over to Christ at that time, but at least there was a small seed planted in them as they saw how my life had so radically changed.

To this day, I still don't preach to my teammates. I'm not one to walk up to somebody and give them the Four Spiritual Laws. But I've had plenty of chances to minister to guys on my team, because from the very beginning it seemed like God gave me opportunities to share my faith through bringing people to me. I still remember the first time that happened. It was the first year I was saved, and somebody asked me a question about the Bible, and I couldn't answer it. I just said, "Let's go to church," and we did. I don't know if that person went on to live a saved life, but I remember that what he heard helped him for that time.

I just didn't have the answers. I was still a new convert who didn't know much of anything about the Word of God. I didn't know what to say to this guy, but I knew someone who did, and he preached at my church. I still don't have all the answers when it comes to spiritual matters, but God still brings people to me so that I can minister to them and pray with them. I have guys coming to me all the time to talk about the Bible, about marriage, about a life decision. And I still love the opportunity to let God use me in people's lives like that.

When I talk to someone on my team who is going through some of the things that I myself went through, I always try to make sure that I don't do it in a judgmental way. I let that person know that I understand where they're coming from because I've been there myself. I tell them that I, too, went through a time when I wasted my money, my time, and my energy on living hard and fast. I tell them what I went through, but I let them know that God has saved me and cleansed me of all that junk, and that He can do it for them, too. After that, I leave it alone. If the person approaches me later to follow up on something we talked about, then I'll do it.

I don't try to get pushy with my teammates, and I don't try to bombard them with the Word of God. Someone has said that the Word makes a great sword but a lousy club, and I think that's true. So when I have an opportunity to talk to my teammates about the Lord, I do it gently, understanding that the young man I'm talking to may be going through something that is even worse than what I endured during "the Mess."

Pursuing Preaching

When I first got saved, I kept myself from any kind of ministry—even with my teammates on the New England Patriots—mostly because at that point I was a baby, and I was advised to start working on my own spiritual life. I was starting almost from scratch, and I had to learn about God, His written Word, how to pray, how to live a holy life, and how to share my faith with other people.

At the same time, though, I had acknowledged my calling from God to preach, and I spent a lot of my time preparing for the ministry I knew was coming in my life. For the next two years, I studied under Rev. William Dickerson of Greater Love Tabernacle Ministries in Boston. At that time in my young Christian life, Rev. Dickerson was everything to me—a brother a teacher, a mentor, a disciplinarian, and a counselor. He taught me everything he knew about how to be a preacher, and I was like a sponge—soaking in everything he told me.

But there was another man who was instrumental in getting me started as a minister of the gospel of Jesus Christ. His name is Charles Terry, and I met him during the off-season following the 1992 National Football League season.

Jacqui, the kids, and I moved to Plano, Texas, during the off-season, and that is when I met Rev. Terry, who was the pastor at the Greater New Birth Baptist Church. After I met Charles, we started to become friends, and I told him what had happened to me in Boston the year before. I told him about my former life, how I'd run from God for all those years, and about how I had gotten saved and had acknowledged God's calling on my life to preach.

It was that year in Texas when Rev. Terry licensed me as a Baptist preacher.

In my church in Boston, I was required to finish two years of study under Charles Dickerson before I could be licensed as a Pentecostal minister, but in the Baptist Church, all I had to do was prepare and give a trial sermon at a church service. (To me, there's not a whole lot of difference between preaching for Baptists or Pentecostals. One service is just a little louder than the other.)

I prepared my sermon, and on July 5, 1992, I stood up before a congregation and preached for the first time in my life.

There were about 200 people in the church when I delivered my first sermon. I'll never forget the strange mixture of nervousness and peace I felt as the time drew near for me to step behind the pulpit. I was more nervous than I'd ever been for anything, even when I first stepped onto the field at the University of Nebraska to play in front of more than 73,000 people at Memorial Stadium. I remembered how my knees were almost knocking that day when I stepped onto the field, how I thought, *Just don't mess this up!*

But this was worse, because I realized how serious it was. I was nervous because I was dealing with the Word of God, with eternal life. This was the real deal, and I didn't want to mess it up. I wanted to preach, and I wanted to preach well. I took what I was doing that day very, very seriously.

Although I was nervous, there was a peace beneath all that nervousness, because I knew that I was doing what God had called me to do. I knew that whatever I said or how I said it, the Lord was in it, so all I had to do was relax and rely on Him to give me the right words to say. I had prepared my sermon, bathed it in prayer, and talked to Rev. Terry about it. I was nothing that day if I wasn't prepared.

I preached that day using a sermon I had titled "Where is your mind?" The text that day was Romans 12:2, which says, "Do not conform any longer to the pattern of this world, but be transformed by the renewing of your mind. Then you will be able to test and approve what God's will is—his good, pleasing and perfect will." It was one of the few Bible verses that I knew then.

The basic theme of my sermon had to do with the things we put in our minds. I asked the congregation: *What kinds of things do you think on? What kinds of things do you put in your mind? What kinds of things do you read? Do you read the things of the world or look at the things of the world? Or do you put your mind on the things of God?* I preached that the things that we put in our hearts and minds are the things that will decide whether we conform to the world or to the Word.

Since I preached my first sermon, I've been licensed as a Pentecostal preacher, following my completion of two years of study and discipleship under Rev. Dickerson.

Because I'm still playing football—currently for the Philadelphia Eagles—I preach mostly during the off-season with a few opportunities coming during the regular season. That's why I say that although I started preaching six years ago, I've only been preaching for three.

I've seen God do some amazing things when I've preached. I remember one time a couple of years ago when I preached in New York City, I gave my testimony and preached from the Bible, and about 250 people came forward to receive Christ. Two other times—once in Florida and once in Philadelphia—I preached, and 150 people came forward. It's almost unbelievable to me that God could use me to speak and that so many people would be moved to give their lives to Christ. I'm not just talking about sports fans, either. I'm talking about people who don't even know who I am, people who have never watched an NFL game in their lives, people who have nothing in common with me.

That's how I know that what God is doing in my life is real, and it's where I get more confirmation that God wants me to preach (not that I need any more confirmation). That's what makes this preaching worthwhile to me. It's been said that angels in heaven rejoice when there is a soul saved. Well, I don't have to wait to get to heaven to hear that rejoicing, because I'm doing plenty of rejoicing on my own when I see people come to the altar to give their lives to Jesus.

A Football Player-Evangelist

I'm asked from time to time if I plan to take on a church and be a pastor when I'm done playing football. Right now, I have to say that the answer to that is "No." At this point, I consider myself more of an evangelist than a pastor.

A lot of people have told me that I would make a good pastor. In fact, some have even said it to me prophecy-style, as in, "You're going to be a pastor." But God hasn't told me that, and that's not my preference. I'm not saying I wouldn't do it—I ran from God's calling once, and I don't plan to do it again—but I'm also not asking God to give me a church to pastor. But if He tells me to be a pastor at some point in the future, than a pastor is what I'll be.

Right now, I'm happy working as a part-time evangelist and serving as an associate pastor at my home church, Hopewell Missionary Baptist Church in Pompano Beach, Florida. It's a nice church with a great mixture of older people, younger people, and family people. About 1,200 people attend the church, which is pastored by Pastor Robert C. Stanley.

But whether God has me working as a pastor or as an evangelist, I want to preach Jesus Christ. I don't care how much I preach, what topics I use, or what Bible texts I preach from—to me it all boils down to one thing: preaching Jesus Christ.

And I'll do that as long as there are people to preach to and as long as I have breath to speak. And I'm happy to do it, too. I'm happy that God has given me this responsibility. I'm glad that He gave me this calling.

CHAPTER NINE

ON-FIELD BLESSINGS

TAKING JESUS TO THE NFL

During the years leading up to my salvation, I tried everything I could to get out of New England. It was nothing against the people in the area, and it wasn't so much the Patriots organization that I wanted to get away from, I just wanted to get away from my problems and the constant negative attention I was then getting.

To tell you the truth, I think the feelings were mutual. I think if you'd taken a poll of the Patriots' fans back then, they would have voted to send me out of town. In fact, they would have helped me pack my bags.

But Coach Raymond Berry wouldn't let me go. No matter how many times I asked to be traded, he hung in there with me. He kept me on the team, kept playing me, and wouldn't let me go to another team, even after my contract with the Patriots expired.

I was in a situation any young receiver would have loved to be in. My head coach was one of the greatest receivers in the history of professional football, and Harold Jackson, the Patriots' receivers coach, was himself an all-time great. Plus, I was playing with Stanley Morgan, who was one of the best in the game when he played. Without fully realizing it, I learned a lot from those men. I soaked up a lot of knowledge and experience from them, and that would be a great help to me later on in my career.

But still, I wanted out. I wanted to leave, and I didn't care how it happened.

After I got saved, things changed. My attitude changed. I decided I was just going to be content playing in New England and let God take care of moving me if that was His will. Not only that, but I became something of a model citizen around the Boston area. I spoke to youth groups and preached. I worked with community service programs with the Patriots. I did the things that help a player get the reputation as a "role model."

All those things helped me change my reputation in New England, and by the time I finally got traded from the Patriots, it seemed like a lot of the same people who would have been willing to buy me a ticket out of town just to be rid of me all of the sudden didn't want to see me go.

Not only did my reputation—and my behavior—improve during that time, so did my play on the field. During the first six years of my career, I was constantly branded with the label *underachiever.* Sure, I played pretty well most of the time during those years. But there was always the feeling among the coaches and the local media that, as the first pick in the 1984 draft, I should be doing more.

There were a lot of reasons I wasn't doing more. For one thing, there was a lot of instability in the Patriots' program then. There were coaching changes, quarterback changes, and changes in our system. But I was part of the problem, too. While I don't think the way I was living necessarily affected me physically, I know it affected me mentally and emotionally. In football, being off balance mentally and emotionally is something you just can't afford.

That all changed in 1991, my first year as a saved man, when I had what was at that point my best season in my eight years as a professional. I caught sixty-eight passes for 1,104 yards (the fact that Hugh Millen came in and had an outstanding year for us at quarterback certainly helped me!) as the Patriots improved from 1-15 the season before to 6-10.

It looked like I had turned around my career, and it looked like the Patriots could be on the upswing as a team. Coach Dick MacPherson, who had come to New England at the beginning of the 1991 season to replace one-year coach Rod Rust, had a positive, upbeat style about him, and a lot of us believed that things were going to get even better in 1992.

But 1992 proved to be almost as big of a disaster as 1990, as we finished 2-14. Dick MacPherson was fired in short order, and the Patriots brought in Bill Parcells to begin a rebuilding job on the team.

It was time for me to get serious about moving on.

"I Don't Want to Stay"

I would be entering my tenth year in the National Football League in 1993, and I didn't want to be part of any rebuilding project. I wanted to go to a team with some stability, a team that had a chance to win. I felt like I was getting too old to start over again, and that's exactly what I was going to have to do if I stayed in New England.

I knew about Bill Parcells' reputation as a coach—how he won two Super Bowls with the New York Giants (the 1986 and 1990 seasons) and that he was considered one of the great coaches of our day. But I also knew that Parcells was going to be the Patriots' fourth coach in five years. I knew it was time to do whatever I could to get the Patriots to trade me.

I didn't make a big stink in the local media about wanting out of New England. I never wanted it to appear that I had anything personally against New England or the Patriots organization, so I made sure that I handled the situation as professionally as possible.

One day, I just walked into Coach Parcells' office and, after exchanging a few pleasantries with him, said, "I don't want to stay in New England. I want to be traded." I let him know that it was nothing against him personally, just that I felt I needed to be playing for a more established team at that point in my career.

Coach Parcells seemed to understand, and said, "I don't want you to stay if you don't want to stay, so we'll see if we can work out a trade for you."

Not long after that, I was on my way to the Miami Dolphins in exchange for a second-round pick in the 1993 draft and a third-round selection in 1994.

One of the things I give God glory for is the way I and the Patriots parted. In a lot of situations like these, there is bitterness and acrimony on one side or the other. But not this time. I had no hard feelings at all. In fact, I was grateful for the opportunities the Patriots gave me to get my career started, and I was grateful that they put up with me during those years when I was an embarrassment to their franchise. I very well could have been out of football by that time in my career, but the Patriots—in particular, Raymond Berry—didn't let that happen.

Now it was time for me to move on, and God put me in just the right place at that time in my life.

Into the Fishbowl

In Miami, I was going to a team that had a great tradition, a great coach (Don Shula, who was inducted into the Hall of Fame in the summer of 1997), one of the greatest—if not *the* greatest—quarterbacks of all time (Dan Marino), and a solid shot to make a run at the Super Bowl.

The Dolphins were coming off a season in which they won the American Football Conference Eastern Division championship with an 11-5 record. They had gone on to beat San Diego in the playoffs before losing to Buffalo in the AFC championship game. Miami had come close in 1992, and I hoped that I could help them take that next step in 1993.

Coach Shula had gone to great lengths during that off-season to upgrade an offense that he felt needed a few more weapons to move the team to the elite level. In 1992 a strong group of rookies joined second-year linebacker Bryan Cox to form a defense that was one of the best in the NFL late in the season and in the playoffs. During that same time, though, the team's offensive shortcomings became more and more apparent. That's why Shula traded for me, signed free agent wide receiver Mark Ingram to a contract, and drafted wideout O. J. McDuffie out of Penn State.

It looked like the Dolphins were loaded and ready for a run at the American Football Conference championship and a spot in the Super Bowl. But 1993, so full of promise even after the midpoint of the season, turned out to be a disappointment in south Florida.

Starting Strong, Finishing Weak

A lot of people wrote off the Dolphins after our October game in Cleveland. That's the game in which Dan Marino was lost for the season with a torn Achilles tendon. We beat the Browns 24-14 that day to go 4-1, but with our leader out for the year, we all knew it was going to be tough keeping up that pace. Surprisingly enough, though, we kept on winning, as Scott Mitchell stepped in and played some of the best football of his career.

We were coming off a 27-10 loss to the New York Jets and had a 6-2 record when we played on a record-setting day at Philadelphia's Veterans Stadium. It was there that Coach Shula—the same Don Shula who led Miami to two Super Bowl wins in the '70s and the famous "perfect season" in 1972—became the winningest coach in the history of professional football.

With Doug Pederson, a third-string quarterback who had once been stuck on the bench on a World League of American Football, taking over for an injured Scott Mitchell early in the second half, we were able to pull out the win, 19-14. We lifted Don onto our shoulders and carried him off the field as the Veterans Stadium crowd chanted, "Shu-la! Shu-la!" Even though its team had lost, the Philly crowd understood that it was witnessing history.

With the win that day, Don had surpassed the legendary George Halas's record of 324 career coaching wins and put himself at the top of the all-time list for wins with 325. I'm still grateful to have been on the field that day.

With Don's milestone behind us, we went on to beat New England 17-13 and Dallas, the eventual Super Bowl champion, 16-14 to go an NFL-best 9-2. But our win over the Cowboys was our last of the season, as we lost our final five games and missed the playoffs. It was a big meltdown for the team, which had played well despite several key injuries during the season but couldn't keep it going during the final five contests.

I was disappointed that we'd missed the playoffs, but I was still happy to be in Miami. The 1993 season was a good one for me personally, as I caught sixty-four passes for 1,010 yards and five touchdowns. I was named as an alternate to the AFC Pro Bowl team, but ended up going to Honolulu for the game when Houston's Webster Slaughter had to pull out due to an injury.

Starting Out Fresh in '94

The off-season after the 1993 season was one in which several key members of the Dolphins took time to recuperate and rehabilitate from injuries. The most notable of those players was Marino, who worked hard and came back ready for a strong '94.

To us, it looked like we would be getting off to a fresh start after a tough 1993.

For me, the first game of the 1994 season wasn't just a fresh start. It was the game of my life up to that point, and it came against my old friends, the New England Patriots. Actually, when I say the "game" of my life, what I really mean is the "half" of my life. I had five catches for an NFL season-high of 211 yards and three touchdowns—all in the second half—as we won 39-35 at Joe Robbie Stadium.

It felt good to have a good game against my former team, and people asked me if it was a day of vengeance for me against the team that had traded me away a season earlier. I didn't look at it that way; I was just glad to be able to do my job—catching passes—and do it well. Besides, there was nothing to get revenge for.

After our opening-day win over the Patriots, we went on to take six of our next eight games to get ourselves a nice 7-2 start. From there, we struggled, losing five of six before our regular season-ending game with the Detroit Lions in Miami. We came into the game needing a win to take the AFC Eastern Division championship, and we got it, beating the Lions 27-20 to finish 10-6 and in first place in the division.

From there, we went on to an AFC wild card game with the Kansas City Chiefs at Joe Robbie Stadium. It was a match-up that featured two quarterbacks who were both destined for the Hall of Fame: Dan Marino and Joe Montana. Statistically, Montana got the better of Dan that day, outgaining him 314-257 in passing yardage. But we came away with a 27-17 win that moved us to the following week's AFC divisional playoff game against the Chargers in San Diego.

We shut down the sell-out crowd at Jack Murphy Stadium by taking a 21-6 halftime lead. The Chargers took control in the second half, and quarterback Stan Humphries gave San Diego the win by hitting wideout Mark Seay with a touchdown pass with 35 seconds left. Pete Stoyonovich's 48-yard field goal try in the closing seconds was wide, and San Diego took the win.

The 1994 season was the best of my career to that point. I finished the season with seventy-three receptions and 1,270 yards, both career highs at the time. I also got to go to the Pro Bowl as a reserve receiver.

A Record Day in 1995

The 1995 season was one in which I was happy to take part in another piece of National Football League history. The day was November 12, the opponent the New England Patriots. The piece of history was Dan Marino's setting a new NFL record for passing yardage, a record I helped him set with a nine-yard reception during the first quarter of the game.

Coming into the game, Dan trailed Fran Tarkenton's all-time passing yardage mark of 47,003 yards. It didn't take him long to put his own name in the record books. The pass came on our second possession of the day. We were facing a second-and-nine situation from our own 39-yard line. Dan called a running play in the huddle, but once he was under center, he saw something in the Patriots' defense that changed his mind. He called an audible for a pass play, one that called for me to run an "out" pattern. Dan took the snap, stepped back a couple of steps, and rifled the ball to me after I'd made my cut.

The record was his.

By the time the game was over, Dan Marino had 47,299 yards and his second record of the season (He also set the NFL record for career completions earlier in the season, in a game against the Indianapolis Colts). After the game, all the media wanted to talk to him about his record, but the only thing he could think about was the outcome of the game: We had lost 34-17, spoiling what had been a record-setting day.

Although I was disappointed that we'd lost, I was grateful to God for allowing me to be a part of setting an NFL record. It's an honor to me to have played with someone who may have been the best to ever play quarterback in the National Football League. I still have a memento of my time playing with him for the Miami Dolphins. It's a watch with an inscription on the back commemorating that record-breaking day:

IRVING,
MY ARM YOUR HANDS
YARDAGE RECORD
47008
THANKS,
DAN
11-12-95

While 1995 was a year of personal records for Dan Marino, it was also a year in which the Dolphins finished below expectations. Coming into the season, we were again picked as one of the contenders for the AFC championship and a trip to the Super Bowl.

We started off strong, winning our first four games. But after a three-game losing streak, we were up and down the rest of the way—winning a few, then losing two more to follow. By the time the season was over, we'd finished 9-7 and in the playoffs as a wild card team. The Buffalo Bills ousted us in short order, taking a 37-22 blowout win at Rich Stadium.

I had a pretty good season my third year in Miami (sixty-two catches for 910 yards and eight touchdowns), but it wasn't up to the standards I'd set for myself the previous two seasons. Although I started all sixteen of Miami's games, I struggled a bit with nagging injuries, and my output showed it.

That season was the last on my three-year contract with the Dolphins, and it was a pretty good three years for me. I'd started all forty-eight games, had two 1,000-yard seasons, averaged better than 1,000 yards a season, and twice made the Pro Bowl.

When the 1995 season ended, the question remained: Would I be back in Miami?

A Change of Scenery?

When I went to Miami, I planned to finish my career there. But there are no guarantees in the NFL, and heading into the 1996 season I had no idea what the Dolphins' plans were for me. Further complicating the picture was the retirement of Don Shula as head coach and the arrival of his replacement, Jimmy Johnson.

Coach Johnson had quickly established himself as one of the best coaches in the business during his tenure in Dallas, where he took a team that was in a shambles and built a mini-dynasty. But he also had a reputation as a coach who liked to build his own team with his own players.

So as the '95 season ended, I was a man without a team. I knew I wanted to stay in Miami. I liked playing for the Dolphins, and there were other things that I didn't want to leave behind in order to sign with another team.

For one thing, I had a good group of Christian brothers with the Dolphins. Keith Jackson, Mark Ingram, Keith Byars, John Kidd, Keith Sims, Richmond Webb, and I were part of a core of Christian guys on the team who prayed for one another, encouraged one another, and had fellowship with one another. We talked about the Lord amongst ourselves and had Bible studies together.

When the team was broken up, it not only broke up our group—a circle of friends and teammates who had a great thing going—but a group who also had a lot of positive influence on the younger guys on the team.

I also had some important things going in the Miami area that were unrelated to football. My family and I attended Hopewell Missionary Baptist Church in Pompano Beach, where I had become an associate pastor. I also started the Irving Fryar Foundation, a non-profit association that raises and distributes money to "at-risk" kids in south Florida.

I also didn't want to move my kids around any more. I'd already moved them once—from New England—and I didn't want to do it again. I knew that I wanted to settle in south Florida, and if I were to sign with another team, that would mean moving my kids back and forth. I hated the thought of doing that to them.

It was hard for me to think about leaving those things behind—even if it were only during football season every year—if I had to sign with another team. I knew that God wasn't finished with me as an NFL player yet, and that He was going to guide my steps. At every step in my life, God had shown Himself faithful, and I knew He wasn't going to stop because of something like an expired contract.

Looking for Work

I left my contract situation in the Lord's hands and waited for Coach Johnson or someone within the Dolphins organization to contact me concerning a new contract. But it didn't happen. Nobody said "We want you back," or "You'd better look for another team," or anything. I was just left hanging. I didn't know what was going on, and it soon became apparent that I had to take it upon myself to go out and find a job.

If I wasn't going to stay in Miami—and it became evident after the '95 season that I wouldn't—there was another place that I wanted to play. It was New England. I hadn't burned any bridges with the Patriots when I left, and I wanted to see if I couldn't get signed with New England and finish up my career there. But I soon found out that God had another plan. I wouldn't be going back to New England. My agent was talking to other teams: San Diego, New Orleans, Tampa Bay, and Philadelphia.

As the off-season wore on, I started to get a little anxious about what was going to happen. There was a lot of free agent movement by wide receivers in the NFL that off-season. Including me, there were eight free agent wideouts who changed teams prior to the 1996 season. New Orleans had lost Quinn Early to free agency and San Diego was looking to replace Shawn Jefferson, so they were the most interested in me. But in the end, Philadelphia, which was looking to replace Fred Barnett (Ironically, Fred had signed with the Dolphins right after the 1995 season), won out. A few other teams had made offers, but I felt that the Eagles had the best chance to be a winner right away. So on March 19, 1996, I signed a three-year contract with Philadelphia.

While I didn't publicly criticize the Dolphins or Coach Johnson when Miami didn't re-sign me, I have to admit that there was a little anger and a little anxiety inside me after everything was said and done. I couldn't understand why, after all I'd accomplished for the Dolphins, they weren't falling all over themselves to offer me a new contract.

But God reminded me of one simple fact: He was in control. He was the One who guided my steps and brought me to Philadelphia. It reminded me of Job 9:12, where he asks, "Who can say to him, 'What are you doing?'" When I gave my life to Jesus Christ that day in the Boston church, I was giving Him control over where I would go, where I would play, and what I would do. As far as I was concerned, He guided my steps to Philadelphia.

God brought me to Philadelphia, and He did it for one reason: to bring people to Himself. I'm committed and submitted to doing what He wants me to do and going where He wants me to go. And however God guides my footsteps, I'm going to do all I can to give Him the glory for the things that happen in my life. I'm going to do all I can to draw people to Him.

God has used me in Philadelphia. He's opened doors to give me opportunities to bring His gospel to the people here. He's even brought glory to Himself through something that at the time I'd rather have avoided. It was an injury I suffered early in the my first season with the Eagles.

I'm Healed!

I hadn't had any major injuries in years heading into my first season in Philadelphia. I'd had the typical bumps, bruises, and muscle pulls that every player in the National Football League deals with every season, and I had been slowed down by some minor problems at different points in my career. But I stayed mostly healthy.

During the entire 1996 season, a season in which I set the Philadelphia Eagles' record for most receptions in a season, I played in some of the most intense pain I had ever felt. It started in our second game of the season—a 39-13 loss to the Packers in Green Bay—when I suffered a stress fracture in my left ankle. From that point on, it was a season of almost unbearable pain for me.

I continued to play and I continued to produce for my team, but I was paying the price with my body. During the week, there were times when I couldn't walk up and down the stairs at home. Every morning, I'd get up and not be able to put any weight on my ankle. It got to where I could barely sleep, and when I did sleep the slightest move by my wife or me in bed would send me out of my mind with pain (Several times Jacqui just got up out of bed and slept on the couch).

Every Saturday morning, I'd get up and not know if I was going to be able to play that week. I never missed a game, though. I'd get a shot of painkiller before the games, then head out and play. But when the shot wore off, the pain would come back worse than ever. As the season wore on, it got to the point where I'd get up at five in the morning and head to the Eagles' training facility to get treatment, and not return home until nine at night. During that time, I didn't see my kids for four or five weeks at a time.

There was never a game during that time when my ankle didn't hurt. As much as the trainers worked on it, as many painkillers as they gave me, it still hurt all the time when I was on the field. To make matters worse, I kept twisting it and aggravating it.

But I couldn't miss a game. As one of the elder statesmen and one of the leaders on our team, I felt like I had to keep playing, even though there were times when I didn't think I'd be able to go on. I wanted to be strong for my teammates, my coaches, my family—everybody. Finally, though, I couldn't take it any more. It was time to do something drastic. I'd tried everything else, so I turned to what should have been my first resort. I prayed. I'm talking about begging-and-crying prayer. I'm talking about the kind of prayer where I'm letting God know that something has to happen—now!

I prayed, "Lord, I'm through with this. You need to do something. Either heal it or finish breaking it, because I can't go on like this. I've got two more games, and we've got the playoffs coming up. If something doesn't happen there's no way I can go on."

Our next game was a Saturday afternoon contest with the New York Jets at the Meadowlands. Before the game, I got two shots of painkiller, and I went out to play. I was ready for more pain, but something strange was happening: My ankle didn't hurt. *I guess it takes two shots to make the pain go away,* I thought. I played the whole game and caught two touchdown passes, including a 14-yarder from Ty Detmer with five and a half minutes to play that proved to be the game-winner for us in a 21-20 win.

The next day, I had the typical soreness that comes after playing an NFL game. All that season, I'd gotten used to dealing with excruciating pain the day after games, but on this day my ankle felt fine. No pain at all. I thought that maybe the ankle was still a little numb from the painkillers. But Monday came, and no pain. Tuesday? Nothing. By Wednesday, I was running up and down the stairs at home just to test it. No pain at all.

I went to the Eagles trainer, James Collins, himself a Christian man, to tell him what was happening. I hadn't said anything to him before he looked at me and said, "You're not limping!" He had this look of disbelief in his eyes. He'd seen me come hobbling into the training room week after week, hurting so bad that I thought I would cry. He'd spent literally hundreds of hours just working on my ankle. Before, when I came in I could hardly walk, but now I was striding around like a teenager. I jumped up and down on my ankle and said, "Look at this! My ankle's healed!" James looked at me and said, "It feels pretty good, does it?"

Did it!? Our last game of the season was against the Arizona Cardinals at Veterans Stadium. I was so hyped up before the game that I didn't care if I caught a pass. All I knew was that I could run full speed, make my cuts, and stop on a dime—all without pain and all without medicine.

Before the game, some of my teammates were looking at the way I was running around and jumping up and down and saying, "What's wrong with you?" and I'd tell them, "Can't tell you right now. You'll find out soon enough."

During the week after our game with Arizona—which we won 29-19—I was approached by reporters from just about every paper in the Philadelphia area asking me how my ankle was. They all had written stories about the pain I was dealing with that season, but they also knew that the pain was now gone. They asked me what I'd done to make my ankle feel better, and I told them: I prayed.

I was able to tell the reporters that I had been healed, that God had taken away the pain. I still remember one reporter's question when I told him what had happened: "It's kind of like that Reggie White thing, isn't it?" Yes it was. It was just like when Reggie had been healed the year before in Green Bay after a severe hamstring pull had him scratched from the lineup for a Packer play-off game. I was able to tell them that the same God who healed Reggie in Green Bay healed me in Philadelphia. I was able to tell them that the God I served and who was looking out for me is the same God Reggie White served.

That week, there were headlines in the Philly area newspapers that read, "Fryar's Miracle," and "Fryar's prayers get answered." Each of the articles that accompanied the headlines quoted me as saying that God had healed my ankle and that He was the reason I was walking and running and leaping without pain.

On Monday one of the local reporters—the same one who asked me about the "Reggie White thing"—came up to me in the locker room after practice and said something that summed up why God had allowed me to endure such pain that season: "I understand what you're saying about God healing you, because I'm a Christian man myself. I appreciate you telling everybody about it, because God can use what you're saying to reach other people." I said, "That's why you asked me about it in the first place. God used you to open the door for me to give the testimony."

He Has His Reasons

So many times, we go through things in our lives that we don't understand, only to find out later that God had a reason for what we were enduring. At first, I didn't understand why God had me move to Philadelphia. And I certainly had no idea why I had to put up with the pain I was feeling for most of my first year there.

But I can look back on the 1996 season and see that God had a plan all along. He had a reason for me leaving Miami—a team I really wanted to stay with—and going to Philadelphia. And He had a reason for allowing me to go through all that pain in my ankle.

It was so that people could see Him in me. It was so that He could increase in the eyes of the people in Philadelphia. I didn't enjoy the fact that I had to leave Miami, and I didn't enjoy the pain in my foot. But I'm grateful for those things now. I'm grateful that God used what was an uncomfortable situation in my life to draw attention to Himself and His power to save and to heal.

Right now, I consider myself a preacher who happens to play football in the National Football League. Some day, I'll be a preacher who used to play in the NFL. But no matter what I'm doing on a full-time basis, I'm committed to allowing God to put me where He wants me to go and having me do what He wants me to do. I know that He can glorify Himself and bring people into a relationship with Him through what I'm doing on Sundays, be it playing football or preaching full time.

Either way, Sunday is my day!

CHAPTER TEN

ACCEPTING A CALLING
GOD CAN DO ANYTHING!

You have a calling on your life.

If you can read this book, if you can comprehend the existence of God, if you can understand who the Lord Jesus Christ is, then *you are called!* You may not be called to be a preacher like I am, and you may not be called to leave home and work as a foreign missionary. But God has a calling on your life, a calling that is as sure and as irrevocable as my calling to preach.

First, you're called to be saved, to come into a personal relationship with the heavenly Father through Jesus Christ. After you're saved, you're called to live a life that is pleasing to God, a life that reflects who you know.

That is a high calling, and what you do with it will determine where you ultimately end up when everything is said and done. With that in mind, you need to realize that what you do with God's calling is the biggest decision you will ever make.

A New Destination

There is one of two places each of us will go after we die: hell or heaven. There is nothing in between, no "limbo" for those who lived a life that was just "OK." You will either spend eternity in horrible torment, or you'll live it in the wonderful presence of the Savior.

When we think of hell, we think of the lake of fire, which is how the Bible describes it (Revelation 19:20). It's a horrible place of suffering that is beyond anything we can imagine. It's a place of hopelessness and darkness, suffering and anguish.

But it's more than that. Hell is a place where it's too late to do anything about your sinful condition, a place where you may call out, "God, help me!" but He won't hear you. While you're alive on earth, you can always call out on God, and, because He's a merciful God, He'll hear you. But when you're in hell, you're there forever, and there's nothing you or anybody else can do to ease the suffering. When you're in hell, you are on your own and God can do nothing at that point to change that fact.

It grieves me to hear people speak lightly of hell or to take that attitude of "My friends will be there too." People who say that have no idea what hell will be like. They don't understand that it is a place where you'll be absolutely alone in your suffering. There have been a lot of jokes told over the years about what hell will be like, but hell is truly no joke. It's an unbelievably horrible place, and nobody who understands what it is like would want to go there.

But the good news is that God never intended for anyone to go to hell. The Bible says in 2 Peter 3:9 that God is, "not wanting anyone to perish...." God wants to save everybody who is willing, and He has made a way for each of us. One way.

It's Jesus.

The Bible says in Acts 4:12 that, "Salvation is found in no one else, for there is no other name under heaven given to men by which we must be saved." If there's a lock on the gates of heaven, there is only one key: the Lord Jesus Christ.

God has provided a way for each of us to escape His wrath and His judgment, and it's the Lord Jesus Christ. There's no other way—not through Allah, not through Buddha, not through Elijah Muhammad. Jesus is the one and only way.

The thing that is most amazing to me about salvation is that it is so simple. If you want to be saved, all you have to do is accept the free gift of salvation from the Lord Jesus Christ, confess your sin, and repent of your sin. If you come to Jesus with sincerity—meaning it in your heart—then you're saved. And when you get saved, you have an inheritance in the kingdom of God. You get to go to heaven when you die. You don't have to go to hell, and you don't have to spend the rest of your life making up for your past mistakes.

You're Invited!

One of the devil's biggest lies is to tell people that they are beyond hope for salvation, that their sins are just too horrible for God to forgive. When someone buys into that lie, they fall into hopelessness and they sink even further into their sinful lifestyles.

Maybe you look at your life and think, *God could never love me! Look how bad I've been! Look at all the mistakes I've made! I'm beyond help, even from God.* If that sounds like you, I know how you feel because I've been there. There have been times in my life where I couldn't believe that God could possibly ever have any use for someone like me.

In human terms, I would have seemed one of the most unlikely candidates for service to God. But, as Jesus tells us in Matthew 19:26, "with God, all things are possible."

There's a story that I love about a little boy who was outside playing one day with his mother. The boy looked up at the beautiful blue sky with the fluffy, white clouds floating around the sun. Suddenly overcome with amazement at the simple beauty of the sky, the boy turned to his mother and asked, "Mommy, who made the sun and the clouds?" His mother smiled and said, "God made them."

That night, as the boy was getting ready to go to sleep, he peered out his bedroom window and studied the nighttime sky with its constellations of stars and the moon. Again, he was astounded at what he was seeing. "Mommy," he said, "who made the stars and the moon?" Again, Mom simply answered, "God made them."

"Wow!" the boy said. "God can do *anything*."

Indeed, He can.

He can even save you.

God has all power in His hands. He's still able to heal the sick, deliver the oppressed, and save the lost. And if God made the heavens and the earth and everything you see—and He did—then He is more than able to save anyone who comes to Him seeking forgiveness and cleansing. And not only is He able to save anyone who comes to Him, but He is also able to use anyone who comes to Him sincerely seeking His will for their lives.

Taking Back the Wasted Years

In the Bible, God says that He can restore the years we waste in our lives through wrong living or through just ignoring Him: "So I will restore to you the years that the swarming locust has eaten, The crawling locust, The consuming locust, And the chewing locust..." (Joel 2:25 NKJV).

If you don't believe that, just look at me. I was as far away from God as I could have been. I was walking in direct disobedience to Him. Yet He saved me, healed me, and cleansed me of the dirt that had stained me for almost the first thirty years of my life. Now I'm preaching the gospel and being used by God to bring other people to Him.

I don't try to sugarcoat anything I did in my past. I was not only on a highway to hell, I was driving a bus full of my friends who were headed there with me. I'm not proud of some of the things I've done in my past. But I'm also not going to sit around grieving over what's been done. There was a time when my life was dominated by deceptions and drugs, and there were times I didn't want to live. I was a mess, and it's a miracle that I'm still here to tell you about it. But I've heard something said that I know applies to me: Without *test* there is no *testi*mony. Those years that were filled with so much garbage for me weren't just something I escaped from or was delivered from. They were also used by God as a way of shaping and trying my faith, which is now more precious than gold and stronger than cast iron.

Now I not only *know* that I'm not going to hell and that I'm going to spend eternity in the very presence of my heavenly Father, I know that while I'm here on this earth, God's going to use me to bring as many people with me as I can. He's going to take the mistakes I made and use the things I learned from them to bring people to Himself. That's how He's restored those years in my life.

Before, I was driving the bus that was taking me and my friends to hell. Now, I'm flying a jetliner to the kingdom of God.

That's the great news in my life. But what's even better news is that God can do what He did in me in *anybody*. I don't care how badly you've messed up, God can take even your worst times and restore them and use them for His own glory. He can bring you out of whatever lifestyle or behavior you've been into and cleanse you, forgive you, and make you suitable for service to Him.

God did that in my life, and He can do it in yours. And there's only one reason for Him doing it: His own grace and mercy.

A Changed Life

It's God's grace and mercy that gives me the peace, that allows me to get up every morning and look in the mirror and know that I have every reason to live and to feel good about myself. It's that grace and mercy that allows me to be able to play with my kids and talk to them and love on them without feeling guilty about something I'd done the night before. It's that same grace and mercy that allows me to sit and talk with my wife and not have to worry about her getting angry with me over something that happened when I was out the previous weekend.

In other words, I'm clean and free of condemnation—all because I know the Lord Jesus Christ as my Savior and Lord.

Satan likes to try to hinder me in my walk with Jesus and my ministry. He just loves to remind me of my old ways and try to make me feel guilty about the things I've done. Sometimes he tries to make me think that all that I've been through was for nothing, that it was just wasted years.

Well, Satan might be selling that load of lies, but I'm not buying it. I know that everything I've done that was displeasing to God is now under the blood of Christ, that He's buried those things in the depths of the ocean, never again to bring them against me. I'm clean. I'm forgiven. I'm headed for heaven when I die, or when Jesus Christ returns.

But there's a paradox to all this, too. While I'm completely forgiven for the things I've done, I'm also able to minister to others because of those things. I'm able to say, "Yeah, I've been through the very things you're dealing with now. Let me tell you, there's a better way. You don't have to waste all your time and money, and you don't have to walk around feeling miserable because you've made a mess of your life. Jesus wants to make a difference. He wants to take those days you've wasted and redeem them and make something good out of them. That's what He did for me, and that's what He can do for you, too."

I know it's hard for a lot of people to understand, but I wouldn't trade my life—my whole life—for anybody's. No, I don't look back on the bad parts of my life with pride, and I wouldn't want to return to that time. But at the same time, I know my testimony can make a difference in people's lives.

Yours can too.

A Call to Live God's Way

If you don't know the Lord, then you need to get to know Him. But if you do know the Lord and you're not living according to His Word—the Bible— then you need to stop wasting time and stop playing with God and start walking in obedience to Him. It's time to get right with God.

I have a couple of things I preach to young people whenever I get the chance, and they have to do with walking the true Christian walk. The first one is, "If you do what's right, you'll be all right," and the other is "Don't pretend to be what you don't intend to be." In short, Don't be a hypocrite! Do it God's way!

Sadly, there aren't a lot of people out there today who are living the Christian life the way the Bible teaches. Too many Christian people are straddling the fence, not able to make up their minds who or what they're going to follow. Still others are doing what they know is wrong, only to come to church on Sunday so they can feel like they're doing what's right at least once in the week.

A tragic example of this is in the divorce statistics. God says clearly in His Word, "I hate divorce!" yet if you look at the statistics, the divorce rate among Christians is about the same as among non-believers. Satan's had his way in our nation's marriages, and that includes those of Christians. Divorce has gone from being a problem for Christians to being the answer for marital problems. What does that say about us as Christians? What does it say about our obedience to the Word of God?

Some Christian folks are doing things wrong and they don't know why they're doing it that way. Why? I believe it's because of their ignorance about the way Satan works. His goal for the Christian is to make that person as weak, sickly, and miserable as possible. He'll do that by any means necessary, but his most common strategy is to keep God's people away from the things that make them strong, namely prayer and Bible reading.

A lot of folks in the church today aren't reading the Bible or praying or fasting like they should. Those are the things that energize us, that give us the wisdom and power we need to do battle with the enemy. They are, as Ephesians chapter 6 puts it, our weapons for warfare against the enemy. But the enemy comes in and takes away those weapons through his own deception, and without them the Christian is helpless against his attacks. When temptations or trials come, the Christian who isn't doing the things he needs to in order to be strong will fall flat on his face.

Today, too many Christians seem helpless against the attacks of the enemy. Obviously, it's time for some changes.

Another thing I preach is this: "If you always do what you've always done, you'll always get what you've always gotten." For example, if I run a perfect pattern in a game but close my eyes when the quarterback throws the ball my way, I'll drop the ball every time. If I continue to close my eyes every time the ball gets there, I'll always get what I've always gotten: a dropped ball. If I want to stop dropping the ball, then I've got to change something. I've got to do something different. I've got to keep my eyes open and focus on the ball. When I do that, I might still drop a ball now and again, but more often than not, I'll make the catch.

As Christians, if we want to make changes in our lives, then we've got to do something different. We've got to make the Word of God—the Bible— and prayer a central part of our lives.

A Call to the Word

I know that if I didn't make the Word a principal part of my walk with the Lord then I'd soon be right back where I started seven years ago. The devil still tries to tempt me with the things that I used to do. But as I stand on the Word of God and on my relationship of prayer with Him, I'm able to repel the enemy's attempts to drag me down. God gives me power through His Word and through prayer, so when the enemy comes to me all I do is what Jesus did when the devil tempted Him in the wilderness. I simply stand on the Word of God, knowing that His Word is more than enough to send the devil scurrying away.

The Bible says in 1 Peter 5:8 that Satan "prowls around like a roaring lion looking for someone to devour." But he can't touch me unless I let it happen, and I'm not going to do that. I'm on to the devil's tactics, and I know that he can't stand up one second to the Word of God.

Just like our bodies need food and water to grow, we need the Word in order to fight a winning battle against Satan. You see, that Word is life. It's power. It isn't just some nice writings by a bunch of religious guys thousands of years ago. It's God's words to His people. It is God's revelation of Himself to us. It is God Himself speaking! And the sooner we realize that the Word is God Himself speaking, the sooner we'll have victory over the devil.

Christian brothers and sisters, read your Bible! Read it, memorize it, meditate on it, and apply it to your life. Fill your heart and mind with the Word, and when you do that you'll have the wisdom and power to send the devil packing.

I love the Word of God. I love to follow David's example in the Psalms where he wrote, "I have hidden your word in my heart that I might not sin against you" (119:11). I hide God's Word in my heart, then I try to live it to a "T." Nobody is perfect in that respect, and I'm no exception. But we are called to obedience to the Word, and we need to make every effort—with the help of the Holy Spirit—to walk in that obedience.

That call to obedience to the Word is absolute, and we are to obey even when other people aren't watching us. The Bible tells us that whatever is done in the dark is going to come to the light. Sometimes you might think you're hiding things from people, but when you stand before God, you're going to have to answer for your actions.

How are we going to know how God wants us to live? By reading the Word and hiding it in our hearts.

A Call to Prayer

Ephesians 6:17 refers to the Word of God as "the sword of the Spirit." If the Word is a sword, then prayer is the source of energy you need to take it out of its sheath and wield it as a mighty, devastating weapon against the enemy.

It's been said many times before, but it's one of the most fundamental truths of our faith: Prayer changes things! When we pray, we move into communication with God and we tap into His unlimited resources of power. When we pray, we put ourselves in the very presence of the Creator of the universe!

Prayer is power. How much power do you want? It's been said like this: "A lot of prayer, a lot of power. A little prayer, a little power. No prayer, no power." It's up to you how much power you have. If you want that power, pray!

Jesus knew the value of prayer. He prayed every day. That was the only way He could have had the kind of power He needed to minister to others. It's the only way He could communicate with His Father in heaven. It's the same with us. Prayer is our source of power and our only way to communicate directly with God. Do you want power? Do you want a stronger relationship with your heavenly Father? Do you want answers to your problems? Pray!

We're God's children. God made us after His own likeness. God wants to hear from all of us. He wants us to talk to Him. He wants to know how we feel. He wants us to seek Him so He can dwell in us and do great things in us.

I'm often asked how we should pray. I believe that we should always approach God first with praise. I always start my prayer times with praise. Sometimes all I do is praise Him. I don't ask him for anything—I don't ask Him to forgive me, to bless me, or to bless my family or friends. I just tell Him, "Thank You for who You are and what You've done for me."

It's easy for me to take that attitude with God, because I remember where I've come from and what He's delivered me from. I can't help but praise God, because I realize what He did to save me, heal me, and make me fit to serve Him. I realize that God Himself paid the price for the life I was living, and for that alone He deserves my undying gratitude and praise.

Repaying God?

We all owe God. I owe God. If you have the ability to comprehend what's around you and inside you, you owe God. We all owe God a debt that we can never repay. But the good news is that He paid that debt Himself when He came to earth in the form of a man and gave Himself up to die in our place as payment for our sins.

How do we repay God for such a marvelous gift? Well, the truth is, we can't. We could work twenty-four hours a day, 365 days a year for the rest of our lives and never repay God for what He's done for us. But God doesn't want your service to Him as repayment for what He's done for you. He doesn't want you to work for Him so that you can feel justified for accepting His free gift of salvation. That debt has already been paid, and anything you do to try to pay it again is worthless service.

Your service to God is to be motivated by your love for Him, by the fact that it is the right thing to do, and by the fact that you want to see others accept the gift that you've already received. That is God's purpose for leaving us here on this earth after we are saved.

We're all called to serve God, and His will for each of us is that we work to bring other people into a saving relationship with Him. We aren't all called to be full-time preachers, pastors, or evangelists, but we're all called to preach the good news of Christ's salvation.

And how do we do that? How do we bring glory to God so that others will come to know Him even if we aren't called to preach? It's simple. In order to fulfill your purpose in Him, you have to do what you do in a way that brings glory to God. Don't do what you're doing just to be doing it, but do it with your best effort possible. Be the best you can be!

I don't play football just to play football, and I don't preach just to preach. I'm not a father just to be a father, and I'm not a husband just to be a husband. I do all the things I do trying to be the best I can in whatever I'm doing. When I play football I want to be the best there is. I don't compete with other preachers when I preach, but every time I step up to the pulpit, I want to give the best sermon I can so that people will see the power of God and come to know Him as their personal Savior. As a father, I want to be the best daddy that anybody could have to my four children. It's the same with my relationship with my wife; I want to be the best husband I can be.

I don't want to be known as or thought of as average in anything I do, be it playing football, preaching, or being a father and a husband. It's been said that average is the best of the worst and the worst of the best. And I know that God doesn't want me to be either. He wants me to be the best I can possibly be in everything I do. He wants me to give my best effort in every area of my life.

The Word says in 1 Corinthians 10:31 that whatever we do, we are to do it for God's glory. That means that we are to do the best we can in all that we do. God knows that we're going to fail at times in things we do. For example, I've had bad football games. I've had sermons where I was a little disappointed in how they turned out. And I've also made mistakes in my relationships with my wife and children. But God is always going to be pleased with us if we give our best effort in what we're doing for His glory.

The great thing about God calling us to be the best we can be in all that we do is that He set the example for us. Whatever Jesus did, He did with the effort befitting His position as the Son of God. There was no halfway efforts from Jesus. From the time He started His ministry to the moment He bid his disciples good-bye and ascended to heaven, He was the best at all He did.

Jesus did this to glorify His Father in heaven, and if we want to glorify God we've got to do the same. God has given each of us a station in life—be it playing football, attending school, ministering to others, being a father and husband, or working a blue-collar job—and we're to look at that station in life as a gift from Him. He gave each of us the abilities we have so that we could use them for His glory.

So, in order to glorify God, you've got to do your best in what you're doing. If you're not doing your best, then you're wasting the talents and skills God gave you, and you're not glorifying God.

When the Praise Starts

When you're the best you can be in what you're doing, there may come a time when someone praises you for your effort or for the outcome of what you're doing. There's nothing wrong with receiving praise from other people, and, in fact, it can give you a chance to let people know what motivates you to give the effort you do. When that happens, you need to let people know that God is your motivation for what you're doing. You need to let them know where your strength comes from and Who gave you the gifts you needed to excel. You've got to give God the glory.

I've received a lot of recognition and a lot of praise for my efforts on the football field over the past several years. Whenever someone says something good about me, I simply say, "Thank you for saying that. I just thank God for helping me succeed, because without His help, I would not have been able to do it." I love to give God the credit and the glory for the things He allows me to do on the football field, at the pulpit, and in my home. I love to do that because I know that if I lift up Jesus Christ, He'll draw people to Himself. I want to bring other people to Jesus. I want them to know Him the way I've come to know Him and to put their eternal lives in His hands so that they can inherit eternal life. That's my calling. And it's your calling too.

EPILOGUE

New Years Day, 1997.

It was three days after my team, the Philadelphia Eagles, had been eliminated from the National Football Conference playoffs by the San Francisco 49ers on a rainy, windy, cold day at the stadium formerly known as Candlestick Park. We'd played a lousy game on offense, losing 14-0 in the wild card game despite a couple of good scoring chances.

I woke up that Wednesday morning, and it seemed like a pretty normal day—except for one thing.

I was crying. I wasn't just a little weepy; the tears were flowing. Something inside me was hurting.

My wife, Jacqueline, woke up to see the tears running down my face. "What's wrong, Irving?" she asked.

No, it wasn't the loss to the 49ers that had me in tears that morning. I was still grieving over that a little bit, but this morning my tears had absolutely nothing to do with football.

It was Gramere.

Alice Oakman, my grandmother, had been dead for six years, but for some reason, that New Year's Day had me in tears because I couldn't go see her that morning.

Grandma and I had made it our own personal tradition when I was a boy to have breakfast bright and early each New Year's Day. She believed that if the first person she saw on New Year's Day was a man, then it would be a good year for her. I always wanted to be that man.

But for some reason, it seemed like the reality of her being gone sunk in to the deepest part of my being that morning. I couldn't believe how much I missed her.

My grandmother was a woman who loved the Lord and loved her grand-kids. And it was she who planted an indestructible seed in my heart and mind that would one day grow and bear fruit as I acknowledged my calling to preach the gospel of Jesus Christ.

But for some reason that only He knows, God took Grandma home to be with Him before she had a chance to hear me preach. She was alive and healthy when I turned my life over to Jesus and acknowledged my calling to preach, but she quietly and suddenly died at the age of sixty-two years.

Grandma's body is buried at a graveyard at the Southern Baptist Church in Aiken, South Carolina. That shell, that earthen vessel that she spent her earthly life in, wore down and expired, but the part of Grandma that will live forever is now enjoying the very presence of her heavenly Father.

Grandma's having a grand old time spending her eternity with Jesus. She doesn't have to worry about any of the cares of this cruel, old world any more. The only thing she has to concern herself with is worshiping God up close with all the saints who have already passed on into His presence.

I know that she's praising God and thanking Him that I'm serving Him as a minister of the gospel. And I know that she has received her reward for being the person who first told me that God wanted me to preach.

And I know she's looking down on me, smiling and cheering me on whenever I step on the football field or up to the pulpit.

AN IRVING FRYAR PROFILE

At Home:

Born September 28, 1962 in Mount Holly, New Jersey to parents David and Ailene Fryar.

Wife: Jacqueline.

Children: two sons, Londen and Irving, Jr., and two daughters, Adrianne and Jacqueline.

Hometown: Weston, Florida.

Home Church: Hopewell Missionary Baptist Church, Pompano Beach, Florida. Irving is a licensed, ordained minister and is an associate pastor at Hopewell.

Received degree in Bible studies on June 27, 1997, from South Florida Bible College and Theological Seminary in Deerfield, Florida.

Formed the Fryar Foundation, a non-profit organization that helps at-risk youths in Florida.

Active in Eagles Youth Partnership, the charitable wing of the Eagles, and was named the team's True Value/NFL Man of the Year in 1996 in recognition of the time and effort he frequently gives to the community.

Hobbies: Irving can play five musical instruments: the drums, trombone, bass guitar, lead guitar, and piano.

In High School:

Attended Rancocas Valley High School in Mount Holly, New Jersey.

Played high school football all four years at Rancocas Valley, earning three varsity letters and being named high school All-American his senior season. Also a standout high school baseball player, Irving was scouted by the National League's Philadelphia Phillies.

In College:

Attended University of Nebraska on full football scholarship. Played on freshman team during 1980 season, when he caught sixteen passes for school-record 432 yards. Averaged 22.3 yards on ten punt returns. Lettered sophomore, junior, and senior years.

All Big-8 his senior season with the Cornhuskers.

Consensus All-American his senior season with the Cornhuskers.

Finished college career fifth on Nebraska's all-time list with sixty-seven catches and second in receiving yardage with 1,196.

Along with Nebraska teammates Turner Gill, Mike Rozier, and Scott Raridon, played in 1984 East-West Shine Game in San Francisco, California. Joined teammates Dean Steinkuhler, Rozier, and Gill in the 1984 Japan Bowl in Tokyo.

In 1993, Irving Fryar was inducted into the University of Nebraska Football Hall of Fame.

COLLEGE STATISTICS*

	Rushing					Receiving			
Year	Att.	Yards	Ave.	TD		No.	Yards	Ave.	TD
1980	2	14	7.0	0		0	--	--	--
1981	7	26	3.7	1		3	70	23.1	1
1982	20	245	12.3	2		24	346	14.4	2
1983	23	318	13.8	2		40	780	19.5	8
Totals	52	603	11.6	5		67	1,196	17.9	11

	Punt Returns					Kickoff Returns			
Year	Att.	Yards	Ave.	TD		No.	Yards	Ave.	TD
1980	0	--	--	--		1	26	26.0	0
1981	24	318	13.3	2		4	55	18.3	0
1982	18	277	15.4	1		4	125	31.3	0
1983	18	113	6.3	0		2	56	28.0	0
Totals	60	708	11.8	3		11	262	23.8	0

All-Purpose Yards				Scoring		
Year	No.	Yards	Ave.	TD	PAT2	TP
1980	3	40	13.3	None	None	None
1981	38	469	12.3	4	0	24
1982	66	993	15.0	5	0	30
1983	83	1,267	15.3	10	2	64
Totals	190	2,769	14.6	19	2	118

1982 Orange Bowl: Passing 1-0-0-0.

1983 Orange Bowl: Rushing 2-12, Receiving 5-84, Punt returns 2-56, Kickoff returns 1-18.

1984 Orange Bowl: Rushing 2-4, Receiving 5-61, Punt returns 3-21, Kickoff returns 2-44.

*College Statistics courtesy of University of Nebraska Sports Information Department.

In the NFL:

Drafted number one overall by the New England Patriots in the 1984 National Football League Draft. Played for nine years for the Patriots before being traded to the Miami Dolphins prior to the 1993 season. Played three years in Miami before signing with the Philadelphia Eagles as unrestricted free agent prior to 1996 season.

Played in Pro Bowl following 1985 season as a kick return specialist, in 1993 as a backup wide receiver, in 1994 as a backup wide receiver, and in 1996 as a backup wide receiver.

Entering 1997 season, Irving is eleventh on the NFL's all-time list for receptions (fifth among active players) with 650 and thirteenth in all-time receiving yardage (fourth among active players) with 10,111.

Irving scored New England's first-ever Super Bowl touchdown in Super Bowl XX against the Chicago Bears.

Irving is the first player in NFL history to record 1,000-yard receiving years with three different teams (New England in 1991, Miami in 1993 and 1994, and Philadelphia in 1996).

Irving became a piece of NFL history when he caught a nine-yard pass from Dan Marino against New England on November 12, 1995, as Marino became the NFL's all-time leader in passing yardage.

PRO STATISTICS#
RECEIVING
Regular Season

Year	Team	G/S	Rec.	Yds	Ave.	LG	TD
1984	NE	14/2	11	164	14.9	26	1
1985	NE	16/14	39	670	17.2	56	7
1986	NE	14/13	43	737	17.1	69t	6
1987	NE	12/12	31	467	15.1	40	5
1988	NE	15/14	33	490	14.8	80t	5
1989	NE	11/5	29	537	18.5	52	3
1990	NE	16/15	54	856	15.9	56	3
1991	NE	16/15	68	1014	14.9	56t	3
1992	NE	15/14	55	791	14.4	54t	4
1993	Miami	16/16	64	1010	15.8	65t	5
1994	Miami	16/16	73	1270	17.4	54t	7
1995	Miami	16/16	62	910	14.7	67t	8
1996	Phil.	16/16	88	1195	13.6	42	11
Totals		193/168	650	10,111	15.6	80t	68

Playoffs

Year	Team	G/S	Rec.	Yds	Ave.	LG	TD
1985	NE	3/2	4	71	17.8	39	1
1986	NE	1/1	2	11	5.5	7	0
1994	Miami	2/2	11	141	12.8	24	1
1995	Miami	1/1	3	29	9.7	15	0
1996	Phil.	1/1	5	62	12.4	20	0
Totals		8/7	25	314	12.6	39	2

RUSHING
Regular Season

Year	Team	G/S	Att.	Yds	Ave.	LG	TD
1984	NE	14/2	2	-11	—	0	0
1985	NE	16/14	7	27	3.8	13	1
1986	NE	14/13	4	80	20.0	31	0
1987	NE	12/12	9	52	5.8	16	0
1988	NE	15/14	6	12	2.0	6	0
1989	NE	11/5	2	15	7.5	11	0
1990	NE	16/15	2	-4	—	2	0
1991	NE	16/15	2	11	5.5	9	0
1992	NE	15/14	1	6	6.0	6	0
1993	Miami	16/16	3	-4	—	2	0
1994	Miami	16/16	0	—	—	—	—
1995	Miami	16/16	0	—	—	—	—
1996	Phil.	16/16	1	-4	—	-4	0
Totals		**193/168**	**39**	**180**	**4.6**	**31**	**1**

Playoffs

Year	Team	G/S	Att.	Yds.	Ave.	LG	TD
1985	NE	3/2	1	3	3.0	3	0
1986	NE	1/1	0	—	—	—	—
1994	Miami	2/2	0	—	—	—	—
1995	Miami	1/1	0	—	—	—	—
1996	Phil.	1/1	0	—	—	—	—
Totals		**8/7**	**1**	**3**	**3.0**	**3**	**0**

PUNT RETURNS
Regular Season

Year	Team	No.	FC	Yds.	LG	TD
1984	NE	36	10	347	55	0
1985	NE	37	15	520	85t	2
1986	NE	35	10	366	59t	1

(Continued from previous page)

Regular Season

Year	Team	No.	FC	Yds.	LG	TD
1987	NE	18	12	174	36	0
1988	NE	38	8	398	30	0
1989	NE	12	1	107	20	0
1990	NE	28	10	133	17	0
1991	NE	2	4	10	10	0
1992	NE	0	1	0	0	0
1993	Miami	0	0	0	0	0
1994	Miami	0	0	0	0	0
1995	Miami	0	0	0	0	0
1996	Phil.	0	0	0	0	0
Totals		**206**	**71**	**2055**	**85t**	**3**

Playoffs

Year	Team	No.	FC	Yds.	LG	TD
1985	NE	6	0	34	12	0
1986	NE	2	0	13	9	0
1994	Miami	0	0	0	0	0
1995	Miami	0	0	0	0	0
1996	Phil.	0	0	0	0	0
Totals		**8**	**0**	**47**	**21**	**0**

ADDITIONAL CAREER STATISTICS: Kickoff returns—1984: 5-95-19.0 Ave.-0 td. 1985: 3-39-13.0 Ave.-0 td. 1986: 10-192-19.2 Ave-0 td. 1987: 6-119-19.8 Ave.-0 td. 1988: 1-3-3.0 Ave.-0 td. 1989: 1-47-47.0 Ave-0 td. 1993: 1-10-10.0 Ave.-0 td. **Totals:** 27-505-0 td.

Career Highs

Receptions: 9 (three times), last at Dallas Cowboys, 11/3/96.

Yards: 211 vs New England Patriots 9/4/94.

Long: 80 yards (for touchdown) from Doug Flutie vs. Chicago Bears

10/30/88; 69-yard touchdown from Steve Grogan vs. New York Jets 10/12/86; 67-yard touchdown from Dan Marino at New England 9/10/95.

Touchdowns: 4, all from Ty Detmer vs. Miami 10/20/96.

#Statistics courtesy of the New England Patriots, Miami Dolphins, and Philadelphia Eagles.

In Select Company

Irving Fryar ranks among the all-time leaders in receptions and receiving yardage. Here are the rankings in receptions and yardage heading into the 1997 season:

All-Time Receptions

1. Jerry Rice 1,050 (12)	**11. Irving Fryar ....650 (13)**
2. Art Monk 940 (16)	12. Charley Taylor 649 (13)
3. Steve Largent...............819 (14)	13. Drew Hill 634 (15)
4. Henry Ellard 775 (14)	14. Don Maynard 633 (15)
5. Andre Reed 766 (12)	15. Raymond Berry 631 (13)
6. James Lofton 764 (16)	16. Sterling Sharpe 595 (7)
7. Charlie Joiner 750 (18)	17. Michael Irvin 591 (9)
8. Gary Clark 699 (11)	18. Harold Carmichael ..590 (14)
9. Cris Carter 667 (10)	19. Fred Biletnifkoff 589 (14)
10. Ozzie Newsome 662 (13)	20. Bill Brooks 583 (11)

All Time Receiving Yardage

1. Jerry Rice 16,377	11. Harold Jackson..........10,372
2. James Lofton 14,004	12. Lance Alworth 10,266
3. Henry Ellard 13,177	**13. Irving Fryar 10,111**
4. Steve Largent 13,089	14. Drew Hill 9,831
5. Art Monk.......................12,721	15. Michael Irvin 9,500
6. Charlie Joiner 12,146	16. Raymond Berry 9,275
7. Don Maynard 11,834	17. Charley Taylor 9,110
8. Andre Reed 10,844	18. Harold Carmichael......8,985
9. Gary Clark.....................10,856	t19. Fred Biletnifkoff..........8,974
10. Stanley Morgan 10,716	t19. Mark Clayton.............8,974

On Eagles' Wings

Irving set a team record for receptions in 1996, grabbing eighty-eight receptions for 1,195 yards and a career-high eleven touchdowns. Here is how his season compares with other great seasons by Eagles receivers:

Greatest Eagles' Receiving Seasons

Player	Year	Rec.	Yards	TD
Irving Fryar	**1996**	**88**	**1,195**	**11**
Keith Jackson	1988	81	869	6
Keith Byars	1990	81	819	3
Fred Barnett	1994	78	1,127	5
Mike Quick	1985	73	1,247	11
Mike Quick	1983	69	1,403	13
Harold Carmichael	1973	67	1,116	9
Fred Barnett	1992	67	1,083	6
Tommy McDonald	1961	64	1,144	13
Harold Jackson	1972	62	1,048	4
Pete Pihos	1953	63	1,049	10
Harold Carmichael	1981	61	1,028	6
Ben Hawkins	1967	59	1,265	10
Tommy McDonald	1962	58	1,146	10

Sharing the Wealth

Heading into the 1997 season, Irving has caught passes from a total of eighteen different players, including sixteen quarterbacks and two running backs. Here is a team-by-team breakdown:

With New England (1984-92):
> Jeff Carlson (1992)
> Tony Eason (1984-89)
> Doug Flutie (1987-89)
> Steve Grogan (1984-90)
> Tom Hodson (1990-92)

Hugh Millen (1991-92)
Tom Ramsey (1985-88)
Marc Wilson (1989-90)
Scot Zolak (1992)

With Miami (1993-95):

Keith Byars* (1993)
Dan Marino (1993-95)
Steve DeBerg (1993)
Bernie Kosar (1995)
Terry Kirby* (1995)
Scott Mitchell (1993)

With Philadelphia (1996):

Ty Detmer
Rodney Peete
Mark Rypien

Of these passers, Irving has caught at least one touchdown pass from all but Carlson, Kosar, and Zolak.

*Running backs.

CORNHUSKER PRIDE

With four National Championships and a streak of twenty-eight straight seasons in which it appeared in a bowl game, Irving Fryar's alma mater, the University of Nebraska, has established itself as one of the very finest college football programs in the nation. Here is some of the lowdown on the Huskers' exploits over the years.

Conference Championships

Missouri Valley—1907, 1910, 1911*, 1912*, 1913*, 1914, 1915, 1916, 1917, 1921, 1922, 1923.
Big Six—1928, 1929, 1931, 1932, 1933, 1935, 1936, 1937, 1940.
Big Eight—1963, 1964, 1965, 1966, 1969*, 1970, 1971, 1972#, 1975*, 1978*, 1981, 1982, 1983, 1984*, 1988, 1991*, 1992, 1993, 1994, 1995.
*Shared conference championship.
#Won title when Oklahoma forfeited three conference games.

Nebraska Record by Decade

The Cornhuskers are currently on pace to make the 1990s their best-ever decade. Here is how Nebraska football fared in each decade since the school started playing football:

Decade	Won	Lost	Tied	Pct.
1890-99	41	25	4	.614
1900-09	70	19	4	.774
1910-19	58	13	6	.792
1920-29	55	18	9	.726
1930-39	62	21	8	.725
1940-49	34	57	0	.374
1950-59	39	58	3	.405
1960-69	75	30	1	.712
1970-79	98	20	4	.820

Decade	Won	Lost	Tied	Pct.
1980-89	103	20	0	.837
1990-96	74	11	1	.866

Going Bowling

As of the end of the 1996 season, the Nebraska Cornhuskers had appeared in thirty-five Bowl Games and had appeared in a bowl game for an NCAA-record 28 straight seasons. Here is a year-by-year listing of their Bowl appearances and the results:

1941 Rose Bowl: Stanford 21, Nebraska 13

1955 Orange Bowl: Duke 34, Nebraska 7

1962 Gotham Bowl: Nebraska 36, Miami, Fla. 34

1964 Orange Bowl: Nebraska 13, Auburn 7

1965 Cotton Bowl: Arkansas 10, Nebraska 7

1966 Orange Bowl: Alabama 39, Nebraska 28

1967 Sugar Bowl: Alabama 34, Nebraska 7

1969 Sun Bowl: Nebraska 45, Georgia 6

1971 Orange Bowl: Nebraska 17, Louisiana State 12

1972 Orange Bowl: Nebraska 38, Alabama 6

1973 Orange Bowl: Nebraska 40, Notre Dame 6

1974 Cotton Bowl: Nebraska 19, Texas 3

1974 Sugar Bowl: Nebraska 13, Florida 10

1975 Fiesta Bowl: Arizona State 17, Nebraska 14

1976 Astro-Bluebonnet Bowl: Nebraska 27, Texas Tech 24

1977 Liberty Bowl: Nebraska 21, North Carolina 17

1979 Orange Bowl: Oklahoma 31, Nebraska 24

1980 Cotton Bowl: Houston 17, Nebraska 14

1980 Sun Bowl: Nebraska 31, Mississippi State 17

1982 Orange Bowl: Clemson 22, Nebraska 15

1983 Orange Bowl: Nebraska 21, Louisiana State 20

1984 Orange Bowl: Miami, Fla. 31, Nebraska 30

1985 Sugar Bowl: Nebraska 28, Louisiana State 10

1986 Fiesta Bowl: Michigan 27, Nebraska 23
1987 Sugar Bowl: Nebraska 30, Louisiana State 15
1988 Fiesta Bowl: Florida State 31, Nebraska 28
1989 Orange Bowl: Miami, Fla. 23, Nebraska 3
1990 Fiesta Bowl: Florida State 41, Nebraska 17
1991 Florida Citrus Bowl: Georgia Tech 45, Nebraska 21
1992 Orange Bowl: Miami, Fla. 22, Nebraska 0
1993 Orange Bowl: Florida State 27, Nebraska 14
1994 Orange Bowl: Florida State 18, Nebraska 16
1995 Orange Bowl: Nebraska 24, Miami, Fla. 17
1996 Fiesta Bowl: Nebraska 62, Florida 24
1997 Orange Bowl: Nebraska 41, Virginia Tech 21

A Fixture in the Polls

Nebraska has been ranked in every weekly Associated Press (Writers) poll since 1981 and has been ranked in the final AP poll for the past 28 years as of the end of the 1996 season. Here is a rundown of the Huskers' all-time final poll positions:

First—1970, 1971, 1994, 1995
Second—1983
Third—1982, 1993
Fourth—1972, 1984
Fifth—1965*, 1986
Sixth—1963*, 1964*, 1966*, 1987, 1996
Seventh—1940, 1973, 1980
Eighth—1978
Ninth—1936, 1974, 1975, 1976, 1979
Tenth—1988
Eleventh—1937, 1969, 1981, 1985, 1989
Twelfth—1977
Fourteenth—1992
Fifteenth—1991
Seventeenth—1950

Eighteenth—1939
Twenty-fourth—1990
*Only ten teams were ranked from 1962-1967.

Nebraska is in a three-way tie for third in all-time national championships with four. Notre Dame leads the way with eight, followed by Oklahoma and Alabama with six each. Minnesota and Miami also have four championships.

Nebraska All-Americans

Any team that has finished in the top twenty as consistently as the Nebraska Cornhuskers will have its share of All-Americans. Here are Nebraska's All-Americans through 1996:

Vic Halligan, Tackle, 1914
Guy Chamberlin, End, 1915*
Ed Weir, Tackle, 1924-25*
Dan McMullen, Guard, 1928
Ray Richards, Tackle, 1929
Hugh Rhea, Tackle, 1930
Lawrence Ely, Center, 1932
George Sauer, Fullback, 1933*
Sam Francis, Fullback, 1936
Fred Shirey, Tackle, 1937
Charles Brock, Center, 1938
Warren Alfson, Guard, 1940
Forrest Behm, Tackle, 1940
Tom Novak, Center, 1949
Bobby Reynolds, Halfback, 1950
Jerry Minnick, Tackle, 1952
Bob Brown, Guard, 1963*
Larry Kramer, Tackle, 1964*
Walt Barnes, Tackle, 1965*
Tony Jeter, End, 1965
Freeman White, End, 1965*

LaVerne Allers, Guard, 1966*
Larry Wachholtz, Defensive Back, 1966
Wayne Meylan, Middle Guard, 1966-67*
Joe Armstrong, Guard, 1968
Jerry Murtaugh, Linebacker, 1970
Bob Newton, Tackle, 1970*
Jeff Kinney, I-back, 1971
Larry Jacobson, Defensive Tackle, 1971
Jerry Tagge, Quarterback, 1971
Rich Glover, Middle Guard, 1971-72*
Willie Harper, Defensive End, 1971-72*
Johnny Rodgers, Wingback, 1971-72*
Daryl White, Offensive Tackle, 1972-73
John Dutton, Defensive Tackle, 1973
Rik Bonness, Center, 1974-75*
Marvin Crenshaw, Offensive Tackle, 1974
Dave Humm, Quarterback, 1974
Bob Martin, Defensive End, 1975
Wonder Monds, Defensive Back, 1975
Dave Butterfield, Defensive Back, 1976*
Mike Fultz, Defensive Tackle, 1976
Vince Ferragamo, Quarterback, 1976
Tom Davis, Center, 1977
Kelvin Clark, Offensive Tackle, 1978*
George Andrews, Defensive End, 1978
Junior Miller, Tight End, 1979*
Randy Schleusener, Offensive Guard, 1980*
Derrie Nelson, Defensive End, 1980
Jarvis Redwine, I-back, 1980*
Jimmy Williams, Defensive End, 1981
Dave Rimington, Center, 1981-82*
Mike Rozier, I-back, 1982-83*
Irving Fryar, Wingback, 1983*

Dean Steinkuhler, Offensive Guard, 1983*
Bret Clark, Safety, 1984
Harry Grimminger, Offensive Guard, 1984
Mark Traynowicz, Center, 1984*
Bill Lewis, Center, 1985
Jim Skow, Defensive Tackle, 1985
Danny Noonan, Middle Guard, 1986*
John McCormick, Offensive Guard, 1987
Neil Smith, Defensive Tackle, 1987
Steve Taylor, Quarterback, 1987
Broderick Thomas, Outside Linebacker, 1987-88*
Jake Young, Center, 1988-89*
Doug Glaser, Offensive Tackle, 1989
Kenny Walker, Defensive Tackle, 1990
Travis Hill, Outside Linebacker, 1992
Will Shields, Offensive Guard, 1992*
Trev Alberts, Outside Linebacker, 1993*
Brenden Stai, Offensive Guard, 1994
Ed Stewart, Linebacker, 1994*
Zach Wiegert, Offensive Tackle, 1994*
Tommie Frazier, Quarterback, 1995*
Aaron Graham, Center, 1995
Jared Tomich, Outside Linebacker, 1995-96*
Aaron Taylor, Center, 1996
Grant Winstrom, Defensive End, 1996
*Consensus Selections

A Pipeline to the NFL

The list of former Cornhuskers who were drafted into the National Football League is long and distinguished. Nebraska has averaged more than five draft picks per season since 1954, and almost seven during current coach Tom Osborne's tenure.

As of 1997, Nebraska has a total of twenty-eight first-round picks all time in the NFL draft. Here are the former Nebraska players who were first-round draft picks:

Year	Player	Pos.	Team	Selection
1937	Lloyd Cardwell	HB	Detroit	N/A
1937	Sam Francis	FB	Philadelphia	N/A
1937	Les McDonald	End	Chicago	N/A
1964	Bob Brown	Guard	Philadelphia	N/A
1964	Lloyd Voss	Tackle	Green Bay	N/A
1972	Jeff Kinney	HB	Kansas City	23
1972	Jerry Tagge	QB	Green Bay	11
1972	Larry Jacobson	Tackle	New York	24
1973	Johnny Rodgers	HB	San Diego	25
1974	John Dutton	Tackle	Baltimore	5
1975	Tom Ruud	LB	Buffalo	19
1979	George Andrews	LB	L.A. Rams	19
1979	Kelvin Clark	Tackle	Denver	22
1980	Junior Miller	TE	Atlanta	7
1982	Jimmy Williams	LB	Detroit	15
1983	Dave Rimington	C	Cincinnati	25
1984	**Irving Fryar***	**WR**	**New England**	**1**
1984	Dean Steinkuhler	OG	Houston	2
1984	Mike Rozier**	RB	Houston	1
1987	Danny Noonan	DT	Dallas	12
1988	Neil Smith	DE	Kansas City	2
1989	Broderick Thomas	LB	Tampa Bay	6
1991	Bruce Pickens	DB	Atlanta	3
1991	Mike Croel	LB	Denver	4
1992	Johnny Mitchell	TE	N.Y. Jets	15
1994	Trev Alberts	LB	Indianapolis	5
1996	Lawrence Phillips	RB	St. Louis Rams	6
1996	Michael Booker	CB	Atlanta	11

*First selection overall.

**Chosen in supplemental draft.

Coaching Success

As of the end of the 1996 season, current Nebraska Coach Tom Osborne has a 242-49-3 record in twenty-four years. Here is a list of the twenty-five all-time Nebraska Coaches and their records:

Coach	Years	Won	Lost	Tied	Win Pct.
E.O. Steihm	1911-15	35	2	3	.913
W.C. Booth	1900-05	46	8	1	.845
Bob Devaney	1962-72	101	20	2	.829
Tom Osborne	**1973-pres.**	**242**	**49**	**3**	**.828**
Fred Dawson	1921-24	23	7	2	.750
D.X. Bible	1929-36	50	15	7	.743
E.E. Bearg	1925-28	23	7	3	.742
W.C. Cole	1907-10	25	6	3	.736
E.J. Stewart	1916-17	11	4	0	.733
Fielding Yost	1898	8	3	0	.727
E.N. Robinson	1896-97	11	4	1	.719
Frank Crawford	1893-94	9	4	1	.679
Charles Thomas	1895	6	3	0	.667
L. McC. Jones	1937-41	28	14	4	.652
Amos Foster	1906	6	4	0	.600
Henry F. Schulte	1919-20	8	6	3	.559
Pete Elliott	1956	4	6	0	.400
Bill Glassford	1949-55	31	35	3	.471
W.G. Kline	1918	2	3	1	.417
George Clark	1945, 48	6	13	0	.316
Bill Jennings	1957-61	15	34	1	.310
Glenn Presnell	1942	3	7	0	.300
Bernie Masterson	1946-47	5	13	0	.276
A.J. Lewandowski	1943-44	4	12	0	.250
A.E. Branch	1899	2	7	1	.250

THE BIBLE TALKS ABOUT
OUR CALLING

Maybe God hasn't called you to be a preacher, but that doesn't mean He hasn't given you a calling. The Bible includes a list of callings that we, the children of the living God, are to acknowledge and live in. Here are some of those callings:

We're called to trust Jesus Christ for our salvation: "Jesus answered, 'I am the way and the truth and the life. No one comes to the Father except through me'" John 14:6.

We're called to repentance: "The Lord is not slow in keeping his promise, as some understand slowness. He is patient with you, not wanting anyone to perish, but everyone to come to repentance" 2 Peter 3:9.

We're called to know God as our heavenly Father: "For you did not receive a spirit that makes you a slave again to fear, but you received the Spirit of sonship. And by him we cry, '*Abba*, Father.' The Spirit himself testifies with our spirit that we are God's children" Romans 8:15–16.

We're called to live a holy life: "Make every effort to live in peace with all men and to be holy; without holiness no one will see the Lord" Hebrews 12:14.

We're called to preach the gospel: "Go into all the world and preach the good news to all creation" Mark 16:15.

We're called to give God our bodies for His use: "Therefore, I urge you, brothers, in view of God's mercy, to offer your bodies as living sacrifices, holy and pleasing to God—which is your spiritual worship" Romans 12:1.

We're called to pray, read the Word, and fellowship with other believers: "They devoted themselves to the apostle's teaching and to the fellowship, to the breaking of bread and to prayer" Acts 2:42.

We're called to minister to our local church body: "Now you are the body of Christ, and each one of you is a part of it. And in the church God has appointed first of all apostles, second prophets, third teachers, then workers of miracles, also those having gifts of healing, those able to help others, those with gifts of administration, and those speaking in different kinds of tongues" 1 Corinthians 12:27–28.

We're called to be led by the Spirit of God: "Those who live according to the sinful nature have their minds set on what that nature desires; but those who live in accordance with the Spirit have their minds set on what the Spirit desires" Romans 8:5.

We're called to praise and worship our heavenly Father: "Come, let us bow down in worship, let us kneel before the Lord our Maker" Psalm 95:6.

We're called to endure persecution: "Blessed are you when people insult you, persecute you and falsely say all kinds of evil against you because of me. Rejoice and be glad, because great is your reward in heaven, for in the same way they persecuted the prophets who were before you" Matthew 5:11–12.

We're called to put Jesus before anything, even our families: "Anyone who loves his father or mother more than me is not worthy of me; anyone who loves his son or daughter more than me is not worthy of me; and anyone who does not take his cross and follow me is not worthy of me" Matthew 10:37–38.